SCAMS, SHAMS, AND FLIMFLAMS

From King Tut to Elvis Lives

SCAMS, SHAMS, AND FLIMFLAMS

From King Tut to Elvis Lives

VOLUME 1

Gordon Stein and Marie J. MacNee

AN IMPRINT OF GALE RESEARCH INC.

Scams, Shams, and Flimflams:
From King Tut to Elvis Lives

Gordon Stein and Marie J. MacNee

STAFF

Kathleen L. Witman, *Assistant Developmental Editor*

Carol DeKane Nagel, *Developmental Editor*

Thomas L. Romig, *U•X•L Publisher*

Barbara A. Wallace, *Permissions Associate*
(Pictures)

Margaret A. Chamberlain , *Permissions Supervisor*
(Pictures)

Mary Kelley, *Production Associate*

Evi Seoud, *Assistant Production Manager*

Mary Beth Trimper, *Production Director*

Mary Krzewinski, *Page and Cover Designer*

Cynthia Baldwin, *Art Director*

Terry Colon, *Illustrator*

Linda Mahoney, *Typesetter*

Library of Congress Cataloging-in-Publication Data
Scams, shams, and flimflams : from King Tut to Elvis lives / Gordon Stein and Marie J. MacNee.
     p.   cm.
   "Volume I"--CIP t.p.
   Includes index.
   ISBN 0-8103-9784-6 (set) : $38.00. -- ISBN 0-8103-9785-4 (v. 1). -- ISBN 0-8103-9786-2 (v. 2)
     1. Impostors and imposture--Juvenile literature. 2. Fraud--Juvenile literature. 3. Swindlers and swindling--Juvenile literature. 4. Deception--Juvenile literature. [1. Impostors and imposture. 2. Swindlers and swindling.] I. MacNee, Marie J. II. Title.
HV6751.S7 1994
363.1'63--dc20

94-15067
CIP
AC

This book is printed on acid-free paper that meets the minimum requirements of American National Standard for Information Sciences—Permanence Paper for Printed Library Materials, ANSI Z39.48-1984.

Printed in the United States of America

Published simultaneously in the United Kingdom
by Gale Research International Limited
(An affiliated company of Gale Research Inc.)

CONTENTS

II
SAINTS, SPIRITS, AND
SUPERNATURAL SCAMS   29

III

HAUNTED HOUSES, CRYPTIC CURSES, AND FORECASTS OF THE FARAWAY FUTURE 61

IV

GLOBE-TROTTING AND GALLIVANTING 77

V

MILITARY MANEUVERS 89

VII
WEIRD SCIENCE, BAD MEDICINE, AND ILLEGITIMATE INVENTIONS 115

VIII
HEROES, BAD GUYS, AND IMPOSTORS   135

IX
YOU CAN'T BELIEVE EVERYTHING YOU READ   171

X
SEEING ISN'T ALWAYS BELIEVING   183

INTRODUCTION

Haunted houses, lake monsters, flying saucers, and deadly death rays. Who hasn't heard of the Bermuda Triangle, the Loch Ness Monster, or the Amityville horror? Yet how many people know the *real* story? Was Silence Dogood Ben Franklin's feminine pen name? Has Elvis Presley booked a return engagement to the world of the living? Is the Loch Ness Monster really an otter? Enquiring minds want to know.

SCAMS, SHAMS, AND FLIMFLAMS BLOWS THE WHISTLE ON 100 HOAXES!

There's no denying it: Weird stuff happens, and sometimes it's *made* to happen. Wouldn't it be great if there were somewhere to find out how The Man Who Never Was managed to fool the Nazis during World War II? How a guy with humongous wooden feet made it look like Bigfoot had been waltzing through the woods? How a psychic "predicted" the president would be shot? If you've got to know how they did it—and maybe even *why* they did it—then look no further: *Scams, Shams, and Flimflams* will tell you everything you always wanted to know about bogus Blue Laws, big-footed beasts, biorhythms, and more.

What exactly is a hoax?

Cons, humbugs, ripoffs, scams, shams, and flimflams—hoaxes by any other name—involve fooling at least *some* people *some* of the time. *Webster's Unabridged Dictionary* (10th ed.) defines a hoax as "an act intended to trick or dupe; something accepted or established by fraud or fabrication." Well, that's a start. Guido Franch was definitely up to mischief when he asked automobile companies to pay him $10 million for a secret fuel formula they could neither see nor test before they paid him. Ben Franklin had a practical joke in mind when he announced—six years prematurely—that a rival almanac writer had died. And Daniel Dunglas Home used more than a little deception to fool people into believing he was floating in thin air.

A successful hoax must be at least a *little* bit believable. Hitler *could* have escaped from his bunker on April 30, 1945. Jack the Ripper *might* have been a doctor who routinely executed the witnesses to a royal scandal. The boy King Tut *might* have cursed all who crashed his kingly catacomb. Then again, maybe not. Often, a good hoax relies on the listener's preconceived notions. Think about it: How many people would have spotted a single sea serpent in Scotland if no one had ever heard of the Loch Ness Monster? Most hoaxes work because *somebody somewhere* is ready, willing, and eager to believe the less than believable.

Does a hoaxer want the hoax to be discovered?

Never; always; sometimes. It depends. Some hoaxes bloom *after* they've been discovered. Take, for instance, George Plimpton's piece about pitching prodigy Sidd Finch that appeared in an April 1 issue of *Sports Illustrated*. The fact is, there *was* no Sidd Finch; that was the point. If no one had discovered that Finch was a phantom, then the article—filled with phoney photographs and bogus biography—would have no point.

At other times, publicity destroys the hoax. Ferdinand Demara, known as "The Great Impostor," had quite a career as a surgeon, a priest, a naval officer, and a number of other occupations that struck his fancy. When *Life* magazine published a portrait of the impostor, however, Demara's career options were soon severely limited.

What isn't a hoax?

Are hoaxes sometimes motivated by financial gain? You betcha. But a hoax—unlike a swindle—is not *based* on the financial return. The master forger Hans van Meegeren, for example, managed to earn a tidy sum by forging the works of famous artists. The money, however, was simply a perk. The second-hand artist had quite another motive in mind: He wanted to force a group of art critics to dine on humble pie—and he succeeded, in spades.

A hoaxer, without exception, *purposely intends* to deceive people. Carlos Allende, who called his UFO stories "the craziest [sic] pack of lies" he ever told, was a card-carrying hoaxer. But not everyone with a wacky take on reality is. Not every tale of Venusian visitors and Elvis encounters is perpetrated by a hoaxer. Some are created by certified cranks—eccentrics who *believe* that what they're saying is *true*.

Not every hoax started out as a hoax. Christopher Columbus had no idea when he died that his grave would inspire centuries of squabbling. Nor did Nostradamus know that his predictions—intended to cover local events in the immediate future—would be used by a Nazi astronomer to predict Germany's victory in World War II. Hoaxes sometimes gather momentum as time goes by.

What you'll find in the books

In two volumes, *Scams, Shams, and Flimflams* offers more than 100 descriptions of well-known hoaxes. The first volume, divided into six sections, includes hoaxes having to do with weird creatures and visitors from beyond; saints, spirits, and the supernatural; curses and predictions; exploration; military maneuvers; and outrageous rules. The second volume, also divided into six sections, includes scores of other hoaxes involving science and medicine; impostors; literature and the arts; entertainment; and sports. Each entry includes interesting background information, an account of how the hoax was played out, how it was discovered, and finally, how it impacted the world. You'll also find 65 photographs that bring the hoaxes to life, and 16 line drawings, too. An index—closing both volumes—provides quick access to names, subjects, and individual hoaxes.

So if you always wanted to be an expert on laws against kissing, if you have a burning need to know about the Hope Diamond curse, or if you just want to read about weird stuff ... inquire within.

Comments and Suggestions

We welcome your comments on this work as well as your suggestions for hoaxes to be featured in future editions of *Scams, Shams, and Flimflams*. Please write: Editors, *Scams, Shams, and Flimflams*, U•X•L, 835 Penobscot Bldg., Detroit, Michigan 48226-4094; or call toll-free: 1-800-877-4253; or fax 313-961-6348.

PICTURE CREDITS

Weird Creatures
and Visitors
From Beyond

Hairy, Two-Footed Creatures

A HOAX
WITHIN A HOAX

Just as the details of the Cardiff giant hoax were coming to light, the New York *Herald* ran a story claiming that the statue had been carved by a Canadian sculptor who thought he was the Michelangelo of his day. Supposedly based on the sculptor's deathbed confession, his story was as phoney as the fossil man.

THE CARDIFF GIANT

The Cardiff Giant—a large stone figure of a human that was supposed to be a fossilized man—is one of the best-known American hoaxes. This is a tale of deceit that spans from New York to Chicago and involves more than a little ill-gotten money.

New York Cigar Maker Unearths Giant Fossil Man!

George Hull, a cigar maker from Binghamton, in upstate New York, had a brother-in-law named William C. Newell, who had a farm near Syracuse, New York, in a town called Cardiff. In October 1869, Hull asked Newell to dig a well on his property, exactly twenty feet behind his barn. This was an unusual place to put the well, but Newell agreed. He hired two local men, and on October 16 they began to dig. Only three feet into the project, their shovels struck stone—the shape of which looked like a huge human foot. Soon, they uncovered the naked body of a ten-foot, anguished-looking stone giant.

Wasting no time, Newell bought a large tent and charged fifty cents per person to view the stone man and hear a fifteen-minute talk. Included in the price was a question-and-answer period for those who required further explanation of the giant's mysterious background.

Business was booming. Even though Newell's farm was not easy to reach, people from all over the northeast took the train to Syracuse, then rode by wagon to the Cardiff bigtop. Soon, stagecoaches ran daily from Syracuse to Cardiff. The giant, still exhibited in the pit where it

was "found," drew an average of 300 to 500 visitors every day (and as many as 2,600 on one Sunday). However, even with $12,000 worth of receipts lining their pockets, Newell and Hull weren't satisfied to let the sleeping giant lie. They sold an interest in the "fossil" to some area businessmen—adding another $30,000 to their growing bank account—and on November 5, the stone man found a new home in Syracuse. Even more people flocked to see the Cardiff giant once the New York Central Railroad arranged a special ten-minute stop so that passengers could step across the street to view the statue.

The experts are fooled. Several experts on fossils and ancient man paid the giant a visit. One of the first, Dr. John F. Boynton, noted that until the Cardiff giant appeared, there had been no earlier evidence to suggest that human or animal flesh could turn to stone. The giant, he concluded, must be a statue that was carved by early Jesuit missionaries to impress the Indians. Professor James Hall, an expert in the study of rock, agreed that the stone creature was indeed a statue.

A sleeping giant.

The local newspapers carried arguments for both sides. Those who opposed the statue theory pointed out that the giant was not supported by a pedestal. They also noted that a naked man writhing in agony was, to say the least, an odd subject for a sculpture. Those who argued the other side pointed to the natural striations (minute scratches in the stone) that indicated the giant had been carved from a single block of stone.

Othniel C. Marsh, a Yale University expert on fossils, took one look at the statue and dismissed it as "a most decided humbug." In his report, he wrote, "It is of very recent origin.... I am surprised that any scientific observers should not have at once detected the unmistakable evidence against its antiquity." Marsh, unlike the other experts, had noticed the fresh tool marks and the presence of smooth, polished surfaces, which would have been roughened had the statue been buried for any length of time. Another look at the statue, and Dr.

Weird Creatures and Visitors From Beyond

Boynton agreed. Soon, the pieces to the puzzle began to fall together.

The genesis of the hoax. In the Book of Genesis, in the Bible, it is written, "there were giants in the earth in those days." After arguing with a clergyman over the meaning of this passage, Hull decided to find a little fun and fortune. He purchased a very large block of gypsum (a mineral suitable for sculpting) from quarry workers in Iowa. Then he secretly shipped it to Chicago, where it was carved by two men (who later confessed to the act). Next, he shipped it by train to a depot near Binghamton, New York. The crate made its way over backroads by wagon to Newell's farm in Cardiff. After the Onondaga County Bank reported that Newell had withdrawn a sizable sum from his account (the payee: one George Hull), people began to remember that, a year earlier, they saw a large, mysterious wooden box being hauled by wagon over the backroads south of Cardiff. Hull had buried the statue behind Newell's farm one year before it was "discovered."

Hull "aged" the stone giant with acid, and created "pores" in the skin by hammering the giant with a mallet studded with needles. The giant's Cardiff burial site was in an area where many fossils and relics—real ones, that is—had been found.

The public remains fond of the fake. The public continued to be fascinated by the Cardiff Giant even after it had been exposed as a hoax. The statue was moved to New York City, where crowds flocked to the Apollo Hall to see it. Moved to Boston, Massachusetts, in February 1870, the giant remained in the limelight. In the following years, the statue showed up at the Pan-American Exposition in Buffalo, New York, and toured in small carnivals and state fairs around the country. In the 1930s, publisher Gardner Cowles purchased the statue, which he kept in his home in Des Moines, Iowa, until the New York State Historical Association finally persuaded him to sell the well-traveled giant. The statue changed hands in 1948, and was transferred to the Farmer's Museum in Cooperstown, New York, where it remains on display.

THE PILTDOWN MAN

Between 1911 and 1915, a jawbone and some skull segments were discovered in Piltdown, England. Supposed to be the remains of a hu-

---

BEATING THE COMPETITION

P. T. Barnum, the founder of the circus in America, offered to lease the Cardiff giant for $60,000. Refused, he had his own copy carved, which he displayed only two blocks from the Apollo Hall, where the original was exhibited. Due to the legendary circus man's promotional skills, the imitation fake drew even more people than the "real fake."

A number of individuals, ranging from fossil collectors to a priest, have been suspected of being involved in the Piltdown hoax. Many of these men were rivals, and any one or a combination of them could have created the scam. Why? Perhaps it was jealousy. Perhaps it was the desire for fame. Perhaps it was a simple desire to sit back and enjoy the show. Among the suspects are:

• Sir Arthur Keith, a famous anatomist (someone who studies the structure of organisms)

• Pierre Teilhard de Chardin, a Jesuit priest and paleontologist (someone who studies fossils)

• Lewis Abbott, a fossil collector

• Martin Hinton, a zoologist (someone who studies animals)

• Arthur Smith Woodward, an anatomist

• Sir Arthur Conan Doyle, a doctor and creator of the Sherlock Holmes character

• Grafton Elliot Smith, an anatomist

• Frank Barlow, a museum technician

• William Johnson Sollas, a geologist (someone who studies rocks)

man-like ancestor of man, the bones were the subject of many books and articles. Today, no one questions that the Piltdown man was created as a deliberate hoax, but *why* a counterfeit ancestor was created is a mystery that remains buried at Piltdown.

Orangutan Jawbone Fools Scientific Community!

In 1953—after the public had been deceived for nearly four decades—Joseph Weiner discovered that the Piltdown Man was a hoax. Weiner, an anthropologist (an expert in the study of human beings), proved that the bones had not belonged to an ancient human ancestor; rather, the Piltdown fragments consisted of part of an orangutan jawbone and a fairly recent human skull.

The list of suspects was long, but most of the evidence pointed to Charles Dawson, who had discovered the first fossil specimens. An amateur paleontologist, Dawson had obtained the specimens either by trading with other collectors or by purchasing them. Together with Lewis Abbott, a fossil collector, Dawson experimented with chemically aged bone specimens. Dawson involved Abbott so Dawson would have someone to accuse if the hoax prematurely came to light.

Dawson went to great pains to make sure that his hoax was not easily discovered. It seems he stole a medieval orangutan jawbone which—after a few adjustments—became the Piltdown Man's fake jawbone. First, he broke off the condyle (where the jaw joins the skull) because it would easily identify the jawbone as that of an ape. Then, he also filed the teeth to make them look human. (Since humans and apes consume different diets, their teeth wear differently.) Lastly, Dawson "aged" the fragments by staining the bone with potassium dichromate (often used as a dye) and treating the unusually thick human skull with other chemicals.

The stage is set. Dawson buried the bones in a gravel pit near Piltdown. He then told a couple of his collector friends that workmen digging for gravel in the pit found an object "something like a coconut." That was all most of the collectors needed to hear: The "Heidelberg Jaw" and other remains of early human ancestors had been discovered

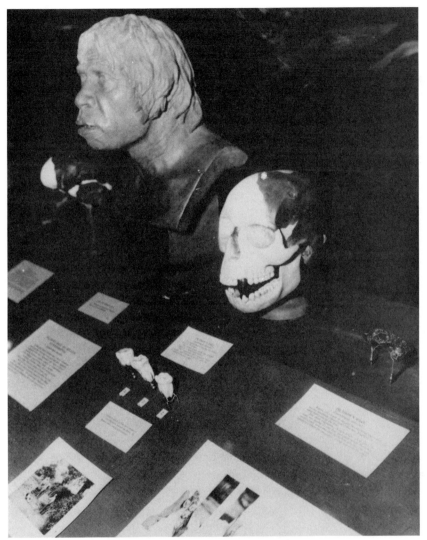

Replicas of the Piltdown Man—labeled an unscrupulous hoax by British scientists—on display in the American Museum of Natural History in New York City.

throughout Europe, but no such fossils had been found in Great Britain. The stage was set for a British find.

Evidence of skullduggery mounts. Dawson acquired a human skull in 1906 and showed pieces of a human skull—probably the Piltdown skull—to others between 1908 and 1911. A little math proves that Dawson's story doesn't add up since the first Piltdown remains weren't discovered until 1911. What's more, sometime around 1910, Dawson asked chemist Samuel Woodhead how to treat a bone to make it appear older. Fossil collector Lewis Abbott then soaked some of Dawson's skull pieces in potassium dichromate "to harden them."

In May 1913, Guy St. Barbe and Reginald Marriot, two amateur archaeologists, observed Dawson experimenting with pieces of bone soaked in chemical solutions. They kept their doubts to themselves, but Weiner's 1953 investigation indicated that not everyone believed in the Piltdown Man. Late in 1913, William King Gregory, an anatomist at the American Museum of Natural History, also voiced doubt about Dawson's remarkable discovery. Although he eventually endorsed the find as genuine, he changed his mind several times about the fossils.

Weiner unearthed the hoax with the help of anthropologist Kenneth Oakley, whose chemical analysis of the bones showed staining by potassium dichromate. The two scientists also discovered that a tooth—which had been found later at the site and was supposed to be part of an elephant molar—was in fact a modern ape tooth that had been painted with brown artist's pigment. Additionally, a "fossil" elephant bone, found later in the pit by workers, had been cut with a steel knife. Steel knives were not used by primitive humans.

Dawson takes his motive to the grave. Why did Dawson bury the fake remains of a phoney prehistoric man? The answer was buried with him when he died suddenly in 1916. Some believe he wanted to be respected as a scientist and accepted as a member of the Royal Society. Ironically, his Piltdown Man remains the longest held and most deceptive hoax in paleontology.

BIGFOOT HOAXES

The existence of a large, hairy, two-footed primate—known as Bigfoot, Sasquatch, Alma, the Yeti, the Wildman, and the Abominable Snowman—remains an unsolved mystery. Reports of Bigfoot sightings, which have come from all over the United States and other countries, are not all hoaxes. Many, however, such as the 1977 sighting of a man in a gorilla suit in Mission, British Columbia, Canada, are bald-faced frauds.

Humongous Feet Leave Trails of Questions!

In the United States, the description of what has been seen or found is fairly consistent. Usually, a sighting reports a seven- or eight-foot-tall biped (a creature that walks upright on two feet) with brownish-red fur (although some reports indicate tan or black fur) and a strong, foul odor.

Footprints have been the most common evidence of bigfoot. In 1982, at the age of eighty-six, Rant Mullens admitted that he had been leaving bigfoot footprints in the Pacific Northwest for some fifty years. A man of modest shoe size, Mullens used bigfoot "feet" carved from wood. The experts, however, aren't buying the hoaxer's story. A foot carved from wood, even if worn as a shoe by a heavy man, will not leave impressions that are as deep or as three-dimensional as the prints that have been found. A number of bigfoot authorities boast of having no trouble recognizing a footprint made by a carved piece of wood.

Wildman Sweeps Woman off Her Feet!

On May 2, 1976, four witnesses said that they saw a large hairy ape-like animal carry off a twenty-three year-old blonde woman from a wooded area outside Eureka, California. According to these witnesses, the animal was, in a word, smelly. The woman—variously identified as Sherie Darvell, Cherie Darvell, and Sherry Nelson—was part of a television crew attempting to film footage of the big-footed one.

The police began their search. If true, this incident would be the first recorded case of the abduction of a human woman by a bigfoot. Two days later, however, the missing woman turned up outside a resort five miles from the site of her supposed abduction. The sheriff, who was not amused, reported that the woman was in good shape but was missing a shoe. The woman did nothing to shed light on her supposed ordeal: According to newspaper reports, when reporters questioned her, she simply screamed. There was no follow-up article, so it is assumed the whole thing was a hoax staged for cameras.

The Iceman Cometh

The "Minnesota Iceman" was supposedly a bigfoot who had been preserved in a block of ice. Exhibited for years in a refrigerated case at small carnivals around the country, the Iceman didn't cause much of a stir; that is, not until biologist Bernard Heuvelmans got wind of the frozen figure. Considered to be the father of cryptozoology (the study of unknown animals), Heuvelmans spent two days with biologist Ivan Sanderson examining the body through the ice. Not easily fooled, he was convinced that the Iceman was an authentic biological specimen, possibly a Neanderthal man.

John Napier, a primatologist (someone who studies primates other than recent man), took one look at Heuvelmans' sketches and notes and concluded that the Iceman was neither a Neanderthal nor a bigfoot, but a fraud.

Frank Hansen owned the Iceman, but his account of where he got it and why it appeared to have been shot through the eye didn't make sense. Gene Emery, on the other hand, uncovered a story that did make some sense. A science reporter for the *Providence* [Rhode Island] *Journal*, Emery discovered that Howard Ball, a modelmaker for Disney Studios, confessed to his wife (who was a widow when Emery spoke to her) that he had created the Iceman at his studio in California. Eventually, Iceman owner Hansen admitted to the reporter that Ball had made an Iceman figure for him.

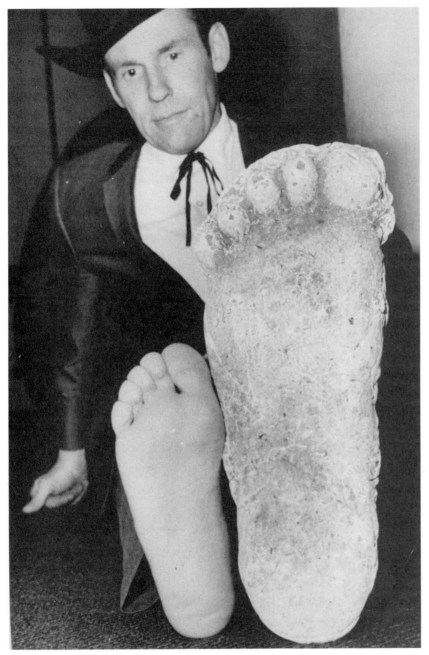

Photographer Roger Patterson compares his foot with a cast he says he made of a big-footed beast near Eureka, California (1967).

Little Bigfoot

"Jacko" was the name given to a small bigfoot that was supposedly captured in 1884 in British Columbia, Canada. The creature—who was four-feet-seven-inches tall and weighed 127 pounds—might have been a chimpanzee, but he clearly didn't belong in the woods of Canada.

Only July 4, 1884, the *Daily British Colonist* published the story of Jacko. The paper claimed that the creature was being held in the local jail until he was to be sent in a cage by train to eastern Canada. That's not, however, the story that bigfoot investigator John Green told. According to an article he found in another newspaper (the *Mainland Guardian* of July 9, 1884), the entire story—including the part that claimed that Jacko could be viewed at the Yale, British Columbia, jail—was a complete hoax. Hoax or no hoax, crowds flocked to the jail to view the creature. This did not amuse the town jailer, who knew nothing about a hairy biped in his quarters. Who was the author of the hoax? Apparently the reporter who wrote the original article.

Big-Footed Woman

Perhaps the most famous bigfoot report that has been called a hoax is the Roger Patterson film of a female bigfoot. Patterson made the twelve-second film in October 1967, near Bluff Creek in northern California. As he rode on horseback in a deep woods, more than twenty-five miles from the nearest road, he spotted a female bigfoot. He leapt from his horse, took his movie camera out of his saddlebags, and managed to shoot thirty feet of film before the creature disappeared into the woods.

The film has been analyzed by all sorts of "experts," whose opinions range from "obvious fake" to "definitely not a man in a monkey suit."

Mysterious Monsters in Watery Places

SEA SERPENT AND LAKE MONSTER HOAXES

For hundreds of years, there have been hundreds of sightings (by experienced sailors) of what appear to be sea serpents. There have also been many sightings of what seem to be very large creatures in Loch Ness in Scotland and in other large lakes all over the world. Many sightings have been discounted as hoaxes; others are mysteries that have yet to be solved....

Terrifying Lake Creatures Lurk in Murky Scottish Waters!

Many Loch Ness "sightings" have been accompanied by photographs. Although it is impossible to say whether all Loch Ness photos are hoaxes, there is no question that some are fakes. Probably the most famous of all Loch Ness monster photos is the one called the "Surgeon's Photo." Robert Kenneth Wilson, a British doctor, took the picture in 1934. Since he did not want his name associated with the photo (a tipoff, perhaps, that a scam was underway), the picture was dubbed the Surgeon's Photo.

The Surgeon's Photo shows what appears to be a neck and some kind of small head sticking out of the water; it also shows a bit of what seems to be the back of the creature. The surface of the water appears to be rippled by small waves, and the creature seems to be breaking the water as it moves. Wilson, who shunned all publicity and all interviews about the photo, never claimed that his photo showed the Loch Ness Monster. The doctor claimed only that the picture he had taken in 1934 was of an object moving in Loch Ness.

Sea serpents— Fact or Fantasy?

BASKING SHARKS AND DUBIOUS DRAWINGS

Sometime in 1809, in Stronsa, an island in Scotland's Orkneys, the dead body of an unidentified creature washed up on shore. What was found on that day has been captured in a well-known drawing, which was believed to depict a sea monster. The carcass was, in fact, the decomposing body of a basking shark. It had decayed to the point that the lower jaw had fallen off, and, as a result, the "creature" appeared to have a long neck and a small head. While the sketch itself was not intended as a hoax, it (and similar photographs) was later published in a number of books and articles. These publications neglected, however, to explain that the creature that looked so much like the fabled sea monster was in fact the decomposing body of a dead shark.

Wilson took the photograph on a quarter-plate camera with what he described as a telephoto lens. At about 7:30 A.M., probably on April 19th, Wilson stopped on the road surrounding the lake. From his vantage point, some 100 feet above the lake, he noticed a commotion about 200 to 300 yards out. Something—he didn't say what—raised what appeared to be its head out of the water. After running back to his car to get his camera, Wilson snapped four pictures of the creature before it disappeared below the water. Only two of the photographs showed anything, one of which was somewhat fuzzy and poorly lit.

The negative of the Surgeon's Photo has been lost and the published versions of the photograph have been drastically cut down in size. Not long ago, however, a man by the name of Stewart Campbell did a thorough analysis of a recently discovered full-original print of the best photo. This picture offered a new perspective on the Surgeon's Photo. Campbell's analysis shows that if the photo were taken from where Wilson says it was, the object is only 0.75 meters (28 inches) long! The photo, Campbell concludes, is probably of an otter's tale; otters, it seems, are quite common in Loch Ness.

Surgeon's Photo a fake. In March 1994, Loch Ness researchers Alastair Boyd and David Martin

Gesner's *Fischbuch*.

announced that the monster in the Surgeon's Photo is a fake. Christian Spurling, the last surviving hoax conspirator, told the two researchers just before he died in November 1993 that the monster was really the head of a fake sea-serpent attached to a toy submarine. Spurling explained that filmmaker Marmaduke Wetherell came up with the hoax, which involved Robert Wilson; Wetherell's son, Ian; and Spurling, Wetherell's stepson. It turns out that the fake "Nessie" was only one foot high and eighteen inches long!

Seasick Sailors Spot Sea Serpent

In 1848, the American brig *Daphne* was unwittingly involved in a sea monster hoax. The master of the ship *Mary Ann* reported that he encountered the *Daphne* just outside Lisbon Harbor (a port in Portugal). The *Daphne's* crew, according to this captain, had just seen a huge sea serpent, which they had repelled by firing spike nails and scrap iron from a deck gun.

The captain's letter was published in the *London Times*. Skeptics soon pointed out that the *Daphne* could not possibly have gotten from the latitude where the serpent was encountered to Lisbon in ten days, unless, of course, the serpent had towed the ship. Yet another newspaper article noted that no ship by the name of *Mary Ann* had been in Glasgow, Scotland, recently, as its supposed captain had claimed. The captain, the *Mary Ann*, and the sea serpent, it seems, were the work of a journalist with a large imagination.

Alien Spaceships and Visitors from Beyond

CARLOS ALLENDE HOAXES THE NAVY

One of the most successful unidentified flying object (UFO) hoaxes of all time was created by an eccentric drifter who sometimes used the name Carlos Miguel Allende. Born in Springdale, Pennsylvania, on May 31, 1925, Carl Meredith Allen spent most of his life wandering the United States and Mexico. According to his family, however, he dwelled permanently in a make-believe world of fantasy. Three items saved Allende from slipping into history unnoticed: two letters to author Morris K. Jessup, and an annotated (marked-up) copy of a paperback edition of Jessup's *The Case for the UFO* (1955).

Pennsylvania Man Encounters Hostile Aliens and Invisible Ships!

Jessup received the first of the letters in October 1955; the second one followed in January. Written in different colors of pen and pencil, and spelled erratically (see quote below), they hinted that the writer—who identified himself both as Allen and Allende—knew all kinds of mysterious secrets about levitation and other matters. These other matters included the Philadelphia Experiment—a 1943 experiment that resulted in

> complete invisibility of a ship, Destroyer type, and all of its crew, While at sea.... Half of the officers and the crew of that Ship are at Present, Mad as Hatters.... The Experimental Ship Disappeared from its Philadelphia Dock and only a Very few Minutes Later appeared at its other Dock in the Norfolk, Newport News, Portsmouth area.... BUT the ship then, again, Disappeared And Went Back to its Philadelphia Dock in only a Very few Minutes or Less.

Gypsy notes of hostile aliens. Jessup assumed that Allende was a crank and thought nothing more about him until a year later, when he received an invitation to the Office of Naval Research (ONR) in Washington, D.C. While there, Jessup learned that in the summer of 1956 someone had mailed an annotated copy of his book *The Case for the UFO* to the ONR office. The notes hinted that the authors, supposedly three gypsies, knew all about the secrets of UFO beings called "S-Ms" and "L-Ms." And they knew that "S-Ms" were hostile toward the human race.

Allende's prank impressed some of the junior officers, who studied the notes carefully; they wanted Jessup's opinion on the foreboding notes about alien creatures. The author took one look at the notes and—thanks to a reference to the invisibility experiment in Philadelphia (among other things)—recognized that Allende had lent a hand in the writing.

The Varo Company of Garland, Texas, ran a small printing of Allende's letters and *Case* notes. The "Varo edition" included an unsigned introduction (written by ONR Special Projects Officers Commander George W. Hoover and Captain Sidney Sherby) that explained, "Because of the importance which we attach to the possibility of discovering clues to the nature of gravity, no possible item, however disreputable from the point of view of classical science, should be overlooked."

A sinister government plot. On April 20, 1959, Jessup, who was troubled over a failed marriage and financial problems, committed suicide in a Florida park. Rumor spread overnight: The author had been murdered by sinister government forces because of what he had learned about the Philadelphia Experiment and other mysteries hinted at in the Allende letters and the Varo edition. Allende's writings—bizarre as they were—soon took center stage as rumor kindled the public's interest.

The legend continued to grow in the 1960s, spurred by numerous publications. A 1968 cover of *New UFO Breakthrough* announced, "Our concept and understanding of flying saucers are totally wrong! So say the bizarre and terrifying ALLENDE LETTERS." The public was hooked. That same year, *The Allende Letters* appeared in a magazine format anthology. In 1974, *The Bermuda Triangle*, a best-seller, and the 1979 book, *The Philadelphia Experiment*, also a best-seller, by William L. Moore and Charles Berlitz, brought the tale to a large popular audience that had never heard it before. Allende's flights of fancy even hit the silver screen, when New World Pictures released *The Philadelphia Experiment* in 1984.

A crazy pack of lies. The legend, it seems, had taken on a life of its own: Allen had admitted to the hoax back in 1969 when he called on Jim and Carol Lorenzen, a Tucson, Arizona, couple who were the directors of the Aerial Phenomena Research Organization (APRO). The Lorenzens, who had never taken the "Allende affair" seriously, were hardly interested in talking to the "legendary" Carlos Allende.

Nevertheless, Allen admitted to them that he, not gypsies, had made the notes in the Varo edition. His written statement said it all: His claims in the book were "false ... the crazyest [sic] pack of lies I ever wrote." Later, however, he changed his mind to say that his confession—not the book—had been a crazy pack of lies.

In 1980, Allen's parents discussed their black-sheep son with writer Robert Goerman, who happened to be their neighbor. They showed Goerman letters in which Carl bragged about his role in creating a modern legend. Carl's brother, Randolph, told the writer that Carl had "a fantastic mind. But so far as I know, he's never really used it." Carl Allen is said to have died sometime in the 1980s.

DREAMLAND—A UFO HOLDING AREA

Area 51, located in a corner of the Nevada Test Site and sometimes called "Dreamland," is said to be the place where work on the secrets of UFO technology is conducted.

Nevada Test Site Harbors Remains of Alien Spaceships!

On November 11 and 13, 1989, Las Vegas's KLAS-TV (an ABC affiliate) carried an astonishing story on its evening news show. The program—the outcome of a one and one-half year investigation by reporter George Knapp—focused on Robert Lazar, who claimed to have been employed at Area 51 in a location designated S-4. Lazar told Knapp that he had been hired by the navy to study some classified technical papers on advanced propulsion systems, and related that he was alarmed to read about systems that were far ahead of anything that could be based on conventional physics. "The power source," he said, "is an antimatter reactor."

Hangars full of alien discs. In due course, Lazar said, he was taken into a hangar where he saw a disc. Although he had been instructed to walk by the craft without looking directly at it, he touched the disc briefly as he passed by. He later saw the object in flight and was allowed to view eight other craft in connecting hangars that were separated by large bay doors. Each craft had a distinctive appearance, but all were disc-shaped.

Lazar's superiors told him nothing about the nature of these discs or about how they had been recovered. Managing to get a glimpse inside one, he saw that "it had really some [small] chairs"—as if the pilots of the craft were of shorter-than-human stature.

A SECRET GOVERNMENT?

"Dark-siders" believe that a sinister "secret government" consisting of the Central Intelligence Agency (CIA), the National Security Agency, and the Council on Foreign Relations runs the United States and murders all those who get in their way—including President John F. Kennedy, who threatened to blow the whistle on them. Dark-siders also believe that this evil American secret government operates in collaboration with the Trilateral Commission and the Bilderbergers, a Geneva, Switzerland, based international secret society. "His Omnipotent Highness Krlll" (pronounced Krill), is the Betelguese ambassador with whom President Eisenhower signed the first human-EBE (extraterrestrial biological entity) treaty. The treaty allowed EBEs to abduct human beings—as long as they were returned to earth unharmed. In exchange, the earth's secret rulers were given the secrets of EBE technology. The extraterrestrials violated the treaty, however, by killing and mutilating some of the abducted earthlings.

The story began to fall together "just all too fast." After having seen the discs in flight, Lazar was convinced that no earthly technology could be responsible for what he had seen. One thing in particular made him certain of his conclusion: He discovered that a substance unknown to earthly science, element 115, played a major role in the development of the gravity-harnessing technology.

The results of Knapp's investigation. During his investigation, Knapp interviewed a "technician in a highly sensitive position," who told him it was "common knowledge among those with high-security clearances that recovered alien discs are stored at the Nevada Test Site."

Lazar's story, however, proved to be somewhat of a mystery for the reporter: Unable to locate documentation to support Lazar's claims about his professional and educational background, Knapp admitted that "checking out Lazar's credentials proved to be a difficult task." Even polygraph tests didn't provide any answers. Nevertheless, Knapp thought that Lazar was probably telling the truth.

Lazar was, for a while, an international UFO celebrity. George Knapp put together a follow-up television special about his story, and he also had dark-sider John Lear on his side. However, his lack of supporting evidence and evasiveness about key issues caused even Lazar's staunchest supporters to doubt his wild claims about the Nevada Test Site. Nonetheless, Lazar has never confessed to making up the story about alien discs at Area 51.

GEORGE ADAMSKI SPOTS VENUSIAN SPACECRAFT

When a Venusian "scoutcraft" landed in a southern California desert on November 20, 1952, George Adamski—a well-known figure in occult circles—communicated with its occupant. Three weeks later, the low-flying scoutcraft passed over Adamski's residence, enabling him to take clear pictures of the alien aircraft. These were hardly Adamski's first flying saucer snapshots; he had been taking them for the past three years.

Man Is Frequent Flyer on Alien Aircraft!

Adamski's account of his experiences was published in 1953 as part of a book titled *Flying Saucers Have Landed*; also included was a manuscript by Desmond Leslie that dealt with spaceships in ancient history and in mystical tradition. The book proved to be tremendously popular and influential. Three years after *Flying Saucers* was published, Adamski

was listed as the author of *Inside the Space Ships* (ghostwritten by Charlotte Blodget). In it, Adamski described his frequent flights in flying saucers and meetings with Venusians, Martians, and Saturnians.

One of George Adamski's UFOtographs, allegedly taken December 13, 1952.

In his book *Inside the Space Ships*, George Adamski described the saucer people he had met. Spiritually and physically beautiful, the "Space Brothers" meant to stop humans from destroying themselves with atomic weapons. Their "cosmic philosophy" was very similar to theosophy, the movement that holds that there is basic truth in all religions.

Most people—including ufologists, who study UFOs—found Adamski's ideas absurd. But he did have his followers, who defended him energetically in books and newsletters. In May 1959, Adamski toured Europe and—despite the disapproval of the Dutch press, the scientific community, and university students (who interrupted one of his lectures with jeers and flying fruit)—he was granted an audience with Queen Juliana of The Netherlands. However, even though he had, indeed, met with Juliana, few people were inclined to believe him when he later claimed to have been called to a secret conference with Pope John XXIII.

A fraud in the making. Adamski's harshest critics were ufologists who believed that the occultist's wild stories hurt their cause. James W. Moseley, the editor of *Saucer News*, dealt a blow to Adamski's reputation by publishing an expose that was based on interviews of people who had been around him during the eventful period in late 1952. One of Moseley's informants, Jerrold Baker, claimed to have seen the model that was used to fake the photographs of the Venusian spacecraft. He also claimed to have heard a tape recording of Adamski and associates rehearsing what they were going to tell the public about an upcoming alien "contact."

A twice-hoaxed tale. Moseley couldn't resist the temptation to hoax a hoaxer. He and a friend, Gray Barker, a UFO and contactee publisher, managed to get copies of State Department stationery, with the department seal impressed on the paper. Using the stationery, they wrote Adamski a letter—from "the Department"—to express their approval of his saucer flights and alien contacts. Adamski believed it; unaware of Moseley's involvement, he tried to get his analysis printed in Moseley's magazine. Moseley declined—and never confessed the hoax until January 1985, one month after his coconspirator Barker had died.

Lost face and wary followers. In 1962, Adamski's alien travels took him a little too far out: Many of his followers found it hard to believe that their leader had attended a meeting on Saturn. They were annoyed at his sudden involvement in psychic practices, an area he had always strenuously criticized. Adamski's reputation suffered another blow when one of his trusted associates, C.A. Honey, caught him in a scam to bilk gullible followers out of money. Adamski, it turned out, was running a for-profit operation on how to contact space people. Nevertheless—despite his supposed trips to Saturn and his designs to profit from space scams—Adamski still had his followers, who believed that their leader had gone astray because he had fallen under evil extraterrestrial, demonic, or even CIA influence.

THE MAURY ISLAND HOAX: THE DIRTIEST HOAX IN UFO HISTORY

In the summer of 1947, unidentified flying objects (UFO) blasted into public consciousness. On June 24, Kenneth Arnold, a private pilot, sighted nine fast-moving disc-shaped objects streaking in formation over Mount Rainier, Washington. In an interview with a newspaper reporter, Arnold described the movement of the flying discs he had seen as saucers skipping over water. The term "flying saucers"—which has survived for almost fifty years—was coined by an anonymous headline writer. Although later proven to be a hoax, Arnold's report sparked a spate of similar sightings.

Witnesses Spot Flying Donuts Near Maury Island!

About three weeks after his June 24 sighting, Arnold received word from Ray Palmer, a Chicago editor. Palmer's publications, two science-fiction magazines called *Amazing Stories* and *Fantastic Adventures*, regularly published material on "true mysteries"—which included what had suddenly become known as flying saucers.

Palmer wanted Arnold to write about what he had seen. In a follow-up letter, he casually asked Arnold if he would look into a story he had heard from one Fred L. Crisman, who claimed to have recovered pieces of a flying saucer. What Palmer didn't mention was that Crisman had approached him before with bizarre stories of alien encounters: Some-

DARK-SIDE MOVEMENT

Where there are tales of aliens and UFOs, there are rumors of conspiracies and cover-ups. The "dark side hypothesis" spells out a sinister government plan: In order to deal with the alien menace without letting the rest of the human race know what was happening, America's secret government needed to raise vast sums of money quickly. It entered into the drug trade, putting a Texas oil company president, George Bush, in charge of the enterprise. In order to reduce the population, the secret government introduced deadly diseases including AIDS. Gun control laws form another aspect of the master plan: With laws to regulate access to guns, criminals (some of whom are trained by the CIA) would have free reign to terrorize law-abiding Americans. Meanwhile, in vast underground tunnels in the Southwest, evil human and alien scientists are tending enormous vats in which soulless android slaves are being created to replace human beings.

A November 1954 edition of the science fiction magazine *Fate*.

DONALD KEYHOE—HOW THE SAUCERS FLY

November 1954 35¢

FATE
ANC
MAGAZINE

BOAC's FLYING JELLYFISH

AIR CHIEF MARSHAL LORD DOWDING "WHY I BELIEVE IN SAUCERS"

time earlier, in a letter, Crisman claimed to have been involved in a gunfight—in a cave—with hostile alien creatures.

Even though Arnold noticed that Palmer "didn't seem to be real cranked up" about the flying saucer story, he flew to Tacoma, Washington, to interview Crisman and Harold Dahl. Identifying himself as a harbor patrolman, Dahl said that on June 21, 1947, he, his son, and two crew members had seen six donut-shaped objects east of Maury Island. One, apparently in trouble, spewed out two kinds of metal—one white and light, the other dark and "similar to lava rock." He also said that he had filmed the objects.

The next day a mysterious stranger, who seemed to know everything about the incident, warned Dahl not to discuss it further. That didn't stop the patrolman from telling Crisman—supposedly his superior in the harbor patrol—who then went to the beach to collect samples. Later, when Arnold inspected one of the samples, he immediately recognized it as lava rock.

Interview with a hoaxer. Arnold was hooked. He contacted a new friend who had recently experienced a much-publicized sighting. United Airlines pilot E. J. Smith flew up the next day to help Arnold interview the two men. After the interview—which took place in their hotel room—Smith and Arnold received a mysterious phone call. A local reporter called to say that someone had called his office and had given a word-for-word report of their secret discussion. Smith and Arnold searched for microphones but found none.

The next morning Crisman and Dahl showed them samples of the lava rock and the white metal. Arnold believed the metal to be "ordinary aluminum which certain sections of all large military aircraft are made of." Slow to suspect a scam, Arnold's confidence was unshaken—even when Dahl said he had given the UFO film to Crisman, who claimed to have "misplaced" it.

Arnold decided that the story was far too big for him and Smith alone. He contacted Lieutenant Frank M. Brown, a military intelligence officer at Hamilton Field in California. Within two hours, Brown—who had investigated Arnold's sighting—flew to Washington, D.C., in a B-25, accompanied by Captain William L. Davidson. As soon as Brown and Davidson saw the fragments, they lost interest, excusing themselves as politely as they could without hurting Arnold's feelings or giving away their conclusions about the rock and metal fragments.

With no further ado, the two boarded their B-25 to return to California. Less than an hour later, the engine caught fire, and both officers died in the resulting crash. The so-called "mysterious" circumstances of the crash became the subject of flying saucer folklore: The two men

EXTRATERRESTRIALS AND ICE CREAM

Rumors of government-extraterrestrial contacts led to an interesting moment on national TV. In 1949, an alien being supposedly survived a crash and was housed at Los Alamos, New Mexico, until it died of unknown causes in 1952. Some people believed that the incident was part of a series of government conspiracies and cover-ups involving aliens and UFOs. Two alleged cover-up insiders, "Falcon" and "Condor," told their stories on a nationally syndicated television show. With their faces shaded and voices altered, they announced a startling revelation on "UFO Cover-up … Live": Extraterrestrials like strawberry ice cream!

had died, some believed, because they "knew too much about flying saucers."

The hoaxers confess. The follow-up air force investigation laid the hoax to rest. Crisman and Dahl—who had made the calls to the reporter's office—confessed that the story was a joke that had gotten out of hand. The air force never officially informed Arnold of its findings, and he continued to believe that the air force was covering up what it knew about the "Maury Island mystery."

In a memoir of his years at Project Blue Book, *The Report on Unidentified Flying Objects* (1956), Captain Edward J. Ruppelt called the affair the "dirtiest hoax in UFO history." Hoaxes comprised only slightly more than 1 percent of the reports in the air force's Project Blue Book files, and many of these involved photographs.

OTIS CARR'S FOURTH DIMENSIONAL SPACE VEHICLE

"I have invented a fourth dimensional space vehicle," New York hotel clerk Otis T. Carr announced in 1957. Shaped like a flying saucer, Carr's vehicle was powered by a revolutionary "Utron Electric Accumulator ... operating in unison with the free energy of the universe." The young clerk, who had befriended the elderly electrical scientist Nikola Tesla, claimed to be knowledgeable about the scientist's many secrets— secrets for which Tesla considered the human race unprepared. Carr, on the other hand, was prepared to reveal the astonishing secrets he had learned ... for a price.

New York Hotel Clerk Shoots for Moon and Lands in Jail!

Carr set up OTC Enterprises in Baltimore, Maryland, in 1955 and secured funding from a prominent businessman in the city. He also hired Norman Evans Colton, a skilled promotion man who sent out a slew of "information bulletins" to investors and other people interested in OTC's projects. The bulletins "explained" the mechanics of flying saucers in clear and easy-to-understand sentences such as these:

> Mount this whole rotating body, with its spindle, on another platform and rotate this platform on a spindle[;] then, if the counter-rotation is greater than the initial forward rotation of the body, a dip-needle on the second platform will point down while the first dip-needle points up, indicating the complete relativity of the polarity. When the exact counter-rotation matches the forward rotation, the body loses its po-

larity entirely and immediately becomes activated by free-energy (tensor stresses in space) and acts as an independent force.

Surprisingly, Carr managed to capture respectful press attention as he discussed his plans to construct a spaceship. The price tag for the OTC-X1—a craft forty-five feet in diameter and fifteen feet high—was to be a whopping $20 million.

OTC Enterprises relocated to Oklahoma City, Oklahoma, where Carr had found some particularly enthusiastic and well-heeled investors. There, he announced his plans for the OTC-X1: On December 7, 1959, he would pilot the spacecraft from the earth to the moon and back. (This was an impressive promise at the time: *Apollo 8*, the first U.S. flight to the moon, would not lift off until December 21, 1968.) Meanwhile, on Sunday, April 19, a six-foot test model would launch its first flight from an Oklahoma City amusement park at three o'clock in the afternoon.

Dad went to see this test model.

A greater scientist than Einstein. Investors assumed that Otis Carr and his public relations man, Norman Evans Colton, knew what they were doing; the duo garnered thousands of dollars in spite of their frequent public blunders. On Long John Nebel's WOR radio show in June 1958, Carr remarked that he could not "even begin to enumerate" the discoveries of Nikola Tesla, the brilliant scientist who was supposed to have been his teacher. Skeptical, a fellow guest asked him to "enumerate just one or two of them," but Carr could only mutter, "That's funny—I cannot remember even one." It seems Carr, who declared himself a greater scientist than Albert Einstein, could not recite even one of Isaac Newton's three laws of motion. Memorizing such things, publicity-man Colton hastily explained, was "a waste of time."

Moon trip leads to jail. Despite the hordes of journalists, curiosity-seekers, and contactees (one of whom swore that "Captain Karnu" and his five invisible spaceships were monitoring the situation), the test was delayed for three days. The test model, it seems, had sprung a "mercury leak." Carr, in the meantime, had come down with a sudden throat ailment, and was conveniently confined to an area hospital.

Three days later the test was called off entirely. Nebel, who had flown down from his New York radio station, demanded to be allowed into the factory where the OTC-X1 was stored. What he saw bore no particular resemblance to an aircraft: He caught a brief glimpse of what looked like a jumble of unconnected parts and wires. Shortly thereafter, a mysterious fire consumed the miscellaneous parts that Nebel had seen.

On May 4, in the county courthouse in Oklahoma City, questioned about stock sales to three wealthy local businessmen, Carr repeatedly took the fifth amendment (refusing to respond on the grounds that his answers might make him look guilty). Two weeks later, Carr, Colton, and two OTC Enterprises salesmen were charged with illegal stock sales. Although Colton had fled the state and was unfindable, Carr was fined $5,000 for a single charge. Since the once-mighty OTC Enterprises had only $1.71 left in its checking account, he was sent to jail to work off the fine at a dollar a day. Carr, who eventually faded from the public eye, died years later in a Pittsburgh, Pennsylvania slum.

A persistent con man. Colton attempted to revive OTC Enterprises—until the New York state attorney general stepped in to stop him. Undaunted, he created the Millennium Agency and sought out customers for "free energy machines ... operated entirely by environmental gravitic forces" which would "draw electricity from the atmosphere without the use of any fuel." Apparently, no one was interested.

Weird Creatures and Visitors from Beyond

Saints, Spirits,
and
Supernatural
Scams

Holy and Unholy Hoaxes

FAITH HEALING

How does the human body sometimes seem to heal itself spontaneously? A number of hoaxers have counted on the fact that people simply don't know. Faith healers claim to be able to heal the ill and the disabled through special powers given to them by God. Whether there really is such a thing as a genuine faith healer, one thing is sure: It's much easier to discover a hoax than it is to prove the real thing.

Faith Healers Work Miracles Thanks to "Dr. Jesus"!

When James Randi, a magician and exposer of frauds, and others decided to investigate faith healers in 1985 and 1986, they limited their study to those who appeared to be employing some form of mentalism. In other words, they targeted faith healers who used the same sorts of "mind reading" tricks that magicians use in magic acts.

On the revival circuit (a series of appearances by faith healers), faith healing is known as "calling out"; in other circles, it's known as a mentalist's routine. The faith healer approaches a person in the audience by name—even though there is no way the healer supposedly could have known the name—and announces the medical problems that afflict that person. The healer often adds personal details, such as the person's address and the names of doctors who have treated the condition. How does the healer claim to know this information? It's passed on, the miracle worker says, from God or from Dr. Jesus.

Investigation targets phony faith healers. W. V. Grant was one of the best known faith healers to employ the hoax of calling out. He and Peter Popoff, another healer who employed this technique, were the main focus of the investigation conducted by the Committee for the Scientific Examination of Religion (with the assistance of James Randi).

The investigation of Grant produced a number of details about his life and his healing methods. Grant claims to have been a star football player in high school, and to have received seventy-seven National Collegiate Athletic Association (NCAA) football scholarship offers; Grant's coach, however, says he didn't receive a single scholarship offer. Grant also claims to have gone to the University of California, Los Angeles, but UCLA has no record of him. As for the doctor of divinity he claims to have received from "Midstates Bible College" in Iowa, it sounds impressive, but no one—including the Iowa Department of Public Instruction, the American Association of Bible Colleges, and the Association of Theological Schools—has any record of the school's existence.

The committee decided to conduct a follow-up investigation of a man who had been cured, according to Grant, by "closed-heart surgery" performed by Dr. Jesus. Six physicians—all named by Grant—had supposedly scheduled this man for open-heart surgery in Georgia, but the investigation found none of these six doctors on the register of Georgia physicians. One of the hospitals mentioned had no record of the patient; what's more, the hospital *never* performed open-heart surgery.

The committee also discovered that a number of people who had been healed by Grant were no better off after Grant had pronounced them "cured." One individual still had a blind eye, another was still totally blind, and yet another continued to suffer from diabetes—but that didn't stop Grant from using pictures of them in his magazine as proof of his power as a miracle healer.

The old wheelchair trick. At each of Grant's services, a number of people sat in the front in wheelchairs. When Grant pronounced them healed, they were able to rise out of their chairs. Apparently, this didn't require much of a miracle: It seems these people had arrived on their own two feet. Grant's organization—which supplied most of the wheelchairs—asked people who *walked* into the auditorium, but who were in need of some type of healing, to sit in the wheelchairs. These wheelchairs were then pushed to the front of the auditorium. People who came in their *own* wheelchairs (and presumably needed them), were wheeled to the rear of the auditorium; oddly, Grant never worked his miraculous powers on those who *arrived* in wheelchairs.

JAMES RANDI PUTS FAITH HEALERS TO THE TEST

In his book, *The Faith Healers*, Randi lists five requirements that must be met in order to prove that a faith healing is genuine.

1. The disease involved must not normally cure itself after a given period of time;

2. The recovery must be complete;

3. The recovery must take place in the absence of any medical treatment that might normally be expected to affect the disease;

4. There must be adequate medical opinion that the disease was present **before** the miracle took place; and

5. There must be adequate medical opinion to verify that the disease is not present **after** the healing has taken place.

The committee looked into the practice of calling out at Grant's rallies. They found that if people went early, they were assured of an aisle seat where Grant could talk to them during the service; this drew a lot of early arrivals. Dressed casually, Grant asked these people questions—finding out their names, the names of their physicians, and their illnesses, so he could decide whom to heal during the service.

Grant also instructed everyone on his mailing list to come early, and to hand their "special offering envelopes" to him personally. As each person came up to the stage to hand Grant his or her envelope—with his or her name written on the front—the wily preacher would stare at them intently for a second or two. This, Randi realized, was no small show of sincerity: Grant was committing each person's name and face to memory.

After receiving the envelopes, Grant retired backstage. There, he opened the envelopes and read each person's "healing cards" in private, memorizing personal details to go with the faces he had committed to memory. Grant may not have been a healer, but he must have had a phenomenal memory—and the notes he concealed in his Bible helped to jog his recollection.

James Randi got hold of some of Grant's crib sheets (notes to prompt his memory), which had been thrown into the trash after one of the services. He also found letters from those who had been "healed," outlining the details of their illnesses. One of the crib sheets said this: "Anthony—deaf in both ears, and bladder and tumors. Connie—pain in left eye and left jaw, thyroid and arthritis. Digestive problems. Bernadette—psoriasis, arthritis. Michael—deaf in left ear. Syl—high blood pressure."

The bug in Peter Popoff's ear. The committee also investigated faith healer Peter Popoff, and what they found alarmed them. Popoff did not associate with his audience before the service. He worked with no crib notes, yet he was able to conduct a smooth "calling out" performance. He seemed to know—without any sort of prior information—people's names and illnesses, and the names of their physicians. He looked like the real thing.

Then one of the committee members managed to get a close look at Popoff during a service: The "healer" wore a tiny hearing aid in his ear. It seems Popoff wasn't exactly hard of hearing. At a later service, an electronics whiz working for the committee managed to sneak an electronic scanner into the auditorium. A search of the frequencies in use in the immediate area soon located a transmitter on 39.17 megahertz that

was carrying the voice of Popoff's wife directly into the minister's ear. Backstage, reading from the "prayer cards," she transmitted information about the various audience members. The committee recorded the transmissions from Elizabeth to Popoff, and Randi later played some of them on *The Tonight Show* with Johnny Carson. Popoff's public was not amused; many TV stations later canceled his services, and the phoney faith healer eventually declared bankruptcy. He did, however, stage a comeback—presumably with no form of hearing enhancement.

POPE JOAN

Some people say that the Pope known as John VIII was really a woman. John VIII—who was supposedly in office for two years, five months and four days, between the years 853 and 855—was probably known as John Anglicus (English John) before becoming pope. In those days, popes did not change their given names.

A depiction of Pope Joan giving birth.

Pope John VIII Was Really a Woman in Disguise!

Though a few sources cite some general references to Pope Joan before the thirteenth century, the first significant reference to her dates to the mid-thirteenth century, about 350 years after she was supposed to have reigned. The *Chronicle of Metz*, provides some telling details about the life of the "popess":

> Query: With regard to a certain pope—or rather popess, because she was a woman who pretended to be a man. By his excellent abilities having been appointed notary at the papal court he became Cardinal and eventually Pope. On a certain day, when he was riding, he gave birth to a child, and straightaway in accordance with Roman justice his feet were tied together and he was dragged for half a league at a horse's tail while the people stoned him. At the place where he expired, he was buried, and an inscription was set up: PETRE PATER PATRUM PAPISSE PODITO PARTUM. [This Peter, the father of fathers, gave birth to a child.] Under him was instituted the fast of the Ember Days, and it is called the popess's fast.

More evidence of a woman pope. The next reference to Pope Joan occurs about fifty years later, in a work called the *Chronicon Pontificum et Imperatorum (Chronicle of Popes and Emperors)*, by Martinus Polonus (who was also known as Martin of Troppau). It says:

Saints, Spirits, and Supernatural Scams

After the aforesaid Leo, John, an Englishman by descent, who came from Mainz, held the see two years, five months and four days, and the pontificate was vacant one month. He died at Rome. He, it is asserted, was a woman. And having been taken by her lover to Athens in man's clothes, she made such progress in various sciences that there was nobody equal to her. So that afterwards lecturing on the Trivium [a group of studies consisting of grammar, rhetoric, and logic] at Rome she had great masters for her disciples and hearers. And forasmuch as she was in great esteem in the city, both for her life and her learning, she was unanimously elected pope. But while pope she became pregnant by the person with whom she was intimate. But not knowing the time of her delivery, while going from St. Peter's to the Lateran, being taken in labor, she brought forth a child between the Coliseum and St. Clement's church. And afterwards dying she was, it is said, buried in that place. And because Lord Pope always turns aside from that way, there are some who are fully persuaded that it is done in detestation of the fact. Nor is she put in the Catalogue of the Holy Popes, as well on account of her female sex as on account of the shameful nature of the episode.

Pope Joan, according to Martin of Troppau, was not included in the list of holy popes because she had sinned *and* because she was a woman.

Old coins tell a different story. A man by the name of Horace Mann believes that there was no woman pope known as Pope Joan. He points out that there are coins that picture Pope Benedict III and the emperor Lothaire together on the same coin. Pope Leo I—who was pope before Benedict—died on July 17, 855, while Lothaire died on September 28, 855. A little simple math makes one thing clear: If Benedict and Lothaire reigned at the same time—as the coin suggests—it must have been during the period between July 17 and September 28, 855. That leaves Joan out in the cold: There was no period between 853 and 855 when she could have been pope. Some people, however, speculate, that the date of Leo's death was later changed from 853 to 855, which brings us back to the possibility that a woman donned the pope's robes between 853 and 855.

The Church responds. The Roman Catholic Church's response to the Pope Joan question has changed over the years. At first, the church seemed to accept the woman pope as real. After the Reformation (a religious movement that modified Roman Catholic doctrine) in the sixteenth century, however, the church began to deny the existence of a woman pope named Joan.

Whether or not Joan was pope, somebody somewhere instigated a hoax. If the woman were indeed a pope, then members of the church have confused the issue. If she were not pope, then somewhere among the people who believe in the woman pope there lives a hoaxer.

VIALS OF TEARS AND CROWNS OF THORNS

Over the centuries, phoney religious relics have been commonplace. The Shroud of Turin is hardly an original: Some forty cloths have been identified as the holy shroud. Fourteen nails have been identified as the nails that fastened Jesus to the cross, when only three or four were supposedly used. Adding to the list of fake relics are vials of Jesus's tears and his mother's milk, countless pieces of the True Cross, and thorns from the Crown of Thorns.

THE SHROUD OF TURIN

The four apostles of the New Testament recorded the existence of a linen cloth used at the burial of Christ after his crucifixion. Many people believe that the Shroud of Turin is that same burial cloth. A number of scientific tests, however, have proven the holy shroud to be a medieval hoax and forgery.

Burial Shroud is Photographic Negative of Crucified Christ!

The cloth—a fourteen-foot sheet of linen that seems to bear the imprints of a crucified man—was first mentioned in about 570 by a pilgrim who said it was kept in a monastery by the river Jordan. About 100 years later, the French bishop Arculph was shipwrecked on the coast of Scotland and traveled to a monastery on the island of Iona. Here he said he saw the shroud and actually kissed it. More references to it appear intermittently until the mid-fourteenth century when it turned up in a small wooden church in Lirey, France. Geoffrey de Charny, a soldier of fortune (for hire), owned the cloth, but was either unable or unwilling to say how he had acquired the fabulous "relic."

Soon after the cloth appeared at Lirey, a scandal was discovered. A report written to Pope Clement in 1389 revealed that the "shroud" was being used to bilk money out of unsuspecting miracle-seekers. Exhibited by the dean of a church at Lirey, the Holy Shroud was being used "to attract the multitude so that money might cunningly be wrung from them." The report further explained that "pretended miracles were worked, certain men being hired to represent themselves as healed at the moment of the exhibition of the Shroud."

Eventually, a bishop "discovered the fraud and how the said cloth had been cunningly painted, the truth being attested by the artist who had painted it." This was all Pope Clement needed to hear. Calling the cloth a painted representation, he forbade anyone to display it as the genuine article.

Saints, Spirits, and Supernatural Scams

The Shroud of Turin is to some a holy relic, to others, a hoax.

The shroud is sold. In 1453, after a century of scandal, Geoffrey de Charny's granddaughter, Margaret, got hold of the shroud. After touring with the "relic" she eventually sold it to the Duke of Savoy. Sometimes portrayed as a religious woman who "gave" the shroud to the duke,

MORE QUESTIONABLE RELICS

Sometime around 620, in Thrace (a region in the Balkan peninsula in southeast Europe), the clothing of the Virgin Mary was "discovered" with no explanation. Pope Gregory (who reigned from 996 to 999) said that he had found Mary's wedding ring in Italy. It didn't seem to matter to him that in the first century, Jewish people did not wear wedding rings. Many churches also had articles of Mary's clothing—including her girdles—among their relics.

Other religious "relics" have been "found":

- The plate on which the lamb was served at the last supper
- The stone on which Mohammed (or Jesus, or Mary) stood while ascending to heaven
- The blood of Jesus
- Letters from Jesus (now lost)
- Clothing of Jesus
- Portraits of the apostles
- Pieces of wood from Noah's Ark

Margaret was in turn blessed with the price of a castle and the revenues of an estate. The church was not so generous and, frowning on Margaret's initiative, ex-communicated her (banned her from the church). This seemed to bother Margaret not in the least, and she died in 1460.

The Duke of Savoy's family—which later became the Italian monarchy—exhibited the cloth, claiming that it was the Holy Shroud and that it had magical protective powers. Magical powers or not, in 1532 the cloth had to be rescued from a fire that destroyed the chapel where it was displayed. A bit of molten silver—from the box in which the shroud was kept—penetrated the cloth's many folds, creating the burn marks and patches that surround the image on the shroud.

Evidence of forgery. When the image on the shroud was first photographed in 1898, the dark and light spots were reversed. People who believed the shroud was real compared the image to a photographic negative, calling it a miraculous "photo" of Jesus. Actually, the image is only approximately negative, since the hair and beard are both positive. The negative impression can be duplicated, it turns out, by taking a rubbing from a raised image (a bas-relief).

Better photographs of the shroud became available in the 1930s. A number of shroud supporters insisted that certain aspects of the image were beyond the knowledge and abilities of a medieval forger. Others disagreed, noting that the footprint on the cloth did not match the image of the leg that belonged to it. And a number of other details didn't add up: The features of the body were unnaturally elongated (strangely similar to figures portrayed in French Gothic art of roughly the same period). The hair fell as if the figure were upright, rather than lying down. And the "blood"—which failed to mat the hair—remained red, unlike old blood, which blackens over time.

From 1969 to 1976, an official committee carried out physical tests of the shroud. When the press found out about the commission—whose members had started out in secret—church authorities of Turin, Italy, denied its existence. Forced to admit that the commission *did* exist, the Turin authorities limited the availability of the commission's report, which

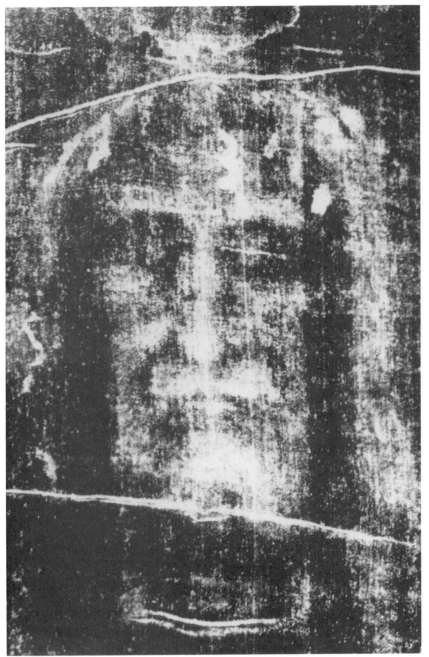

A close-up of the face of Christ as it appears in the Shroud of Turin.

questioned the origin of the cloth and suggested that the shroud was an artistic work made by some imprinting technique. The church's counter response, on the other hand, was available to anyone who showed interest.

The shroud fails a blood test. Two blood experts (forensic serologists) put the "blood"-stained threads through extensive tests. The blood failed all of them. The experts tested for hemoglobin, conducted microscopic examinations to look for blood corpuscles, and performed other analyses using highly technical instruments. What they found didn't look like blood: They reported the presence of a reddish granule that would not dissolve when they tried to analyze it. Yet another expert found what others had suspected all along: He discovered what looked like traces of paint.

In 1978, the Shroud of Turin Research Project (STURP) continued to examine the cloth. Many of the project members, however, had already made up their minds about the shroud's authenticity. STURP's leaders, it seems, served on the Catholic Holy Shroud Guild, whose members staunchly defended the holy shroud as a genuine relic. Still, other STURP scientists revealed that they leaned in favor of the authenticity of the shroud *before they ever examined the shroud*. And the project was hardly an assembly of experts: All but one of the STURP scientists lacked expertise in identifying paint pigments and in detecting art forgeries.

The one exception was Walter McCrone, an internationally famous microanalyst (someone who conducts chemical analysis on very small samples). He performed "blind" studies of samples taken from the shroud, and found significant amounts of the pigment red ocher (red iron oxide) on image areas; he didn't, however, find any pigment on the cloth where there was no image. The blood on the shroud, McCrone found, was nothing more than tempera paint containing red ocher and another pigment, vermillion.

STURP refused to endorse McCrone's report, and held him to a legal agreement not to reveal his results. However, when this "covenant not to disclose" expired, he published his reports, complete with paint globules and pigment particles.

The "experts" lack experience. McCrone—who claims to have been "drummed out" of STURP—was replaced by John Heller and Alan Adler. The two scientists soon claimed that McCrone's findings and those of the commission scientists were inaccurate. They also claimed that they had "identified" the presence of blood on the shroud. It seemed, at first, that Heller and Adler might have discovered something that McCrone had overlooked. But it was their credentials that had been overlooked: Neither scientist was an expert in blood or pigment analysis. Heller admitted that McCrone "had over two decades of experience with this kind of problem and a worldwide reputation." He and Adler, on the other hand, "had never before tackled anything remotely like an artistic forgery."

Another expert by the name of John F. Fischer reviewed Heller and Adler's claims. He found that none of their tests was specific for blood, and that their approach to identifying blood was not scientifically acceptable. In fact, Heller and Adler could have obtained the same results from tempera paint.

In a presentation to the International Association for Identification (an organization of police officials and individuals engaged in forensic sciences, investigation, and scientific crime detection work), Fischer also noted that analysis of the blood produced results that were fundamentally inconsistent with genuine blood.

Three laboratories—in England, Switzerland, and Arizona—used radiocarbon tests to date the shroud. Performing analyses on small swatches cut from the cloth, the three labs produced dates that were surprisingly close. They determined that the cloth had been produced sometime between 1260 and 1390, a time span that coincides with the forger's confession.

PROTOCOLS OF THE ELDERS OF ZION

Some hoaxes are harmless and are conceived in the spirit of humor. The hoax of the *Protocols of the Elders of Zion*, however, was far from harmless, and its conception had nothing to do with humor.

Fake Document Fuels Nazi Furnace!

The *Protocols* has a tangled and mysterious history. Although it is not known exactly how the *Protocols* developed, it appears that the episode began in Paris, France, in 1864. In that year, a political satirist named Maurice Joly published his book *A Dialog in Hell between Montesquieu and Machiavelli (Dialogue aux Enfer entre Montesquieu et Machiavel)*. Although the book was actually published in Brussels, Belgium, its title page said it was published in Geneva, Switzerland.

Joly's *Dialog* openly criticized Emperor Napoleon III—a criminal offense at the time—by putting the emperor's words in the mouths of Machiavelli and Montesquieu, two political philosophers whose theories were out of favor with Napoleon III's government. The book was smuggled into France, but was seized at the border. Arrested and tried, Joly was sentenced to fifteen months imprisonment on April 25, 1865.

> **SATIRE:**
> A literary work holding up human vices and follies to ridicule or scorn; wit, irony, or sarcasm used to expose and discredit vice or folly. (*Webster's Ninth*)

> **ANTI-SEMITISM:**
> Hostility toward or discrimination against Jews as a religious or racial group.

DOG-EARED *DIALOG*

The French national library (Bibliothèque Nationale) has a copy of Joly's *Dialog*. The book has markings that indicate that it was probably the copy used to provide information for the *Protocols*.

PROTOCOLS TIED TO THE DREYFUS AFFAIR

Author Norman Cohn is "practically certain" that the *Protocols* was made up in Paris sometime between 1894 and 1899. That corresponds with the time of the Dreyfus Affair, when a Jewish army captain was accused of treason in an anti-Semitic incident.

After Joly's *Dialog* was banned and copies were confiscated, the book soon became a rare work. Eventually, this rarity would help to hide the fact that the *Protocols* actually lifted large sections of the imaginary dialog from the satirical, and fictional, French work.

In Berlin, Germany, in 1868, Hermann Goedsche, a minor official in the German Postal Service (who wrote under the name of Sir John Retcliffe), published a novel called *Biarritz*. One chapter, called "In the Jewish Cemetery in Prague," describes a secret nighttime meeting held in the cemetery during the Feast of Tabernacles. There the leaders of the twelve tribes of Israel meet with the Devil to report on their activities during the century that has passed since their last meeting.

The leaders report that the Jewish people are making great strides toward taking over the world. Thanks to the stock exchange, they have put all the princes and governments of Europe into their debt. They discuss a scheme to put all lands under Jewish control, and outline plans to upset the Christian Church; they also talk about gaining control of the press, and discuss schemes to land high governmental positions. In short, their quest for world domination is going well. After renewing their oath, the leaders agree to meet again in 100 years.

A completely fictional work, *Biarritz* played on many of the fears that anti-Semites had voiced for hundreds of years.

A Russian conspirator. Pyotr Rachkovsky was the head of the foreign branch of the Russian secret police from 1884 to 1902. He organized the overseas operations of the Okhrana (secret police) in Paris, France (the overseas headquarters); Switzerland; London, England; and Berlin. Rachkovsky was also in charge of transforming the two fictional works by Joly and Goedsche into the *Protocols*.

In 1887, Rachkovsky planted a forged letter in the French press; it claimed the majority of terrorists active in France at that time were Jewish. Five years later, in Paris, Rachkovsy published a book titled *Anarchy and Nihilism (Anarchie et Nihilisme)*, which claimed that the French Revolution made the Jew "the absolute master of the situation in Europe ... governing by discreet means both monarchies and republics." According to Rachkovsky's book, only one thing—the Jewish domination of Russia—was yet to be accomplished. And this, he argued, was already underway.

The *Protocols* was published in America in 1920. That year, Henry Ford's newspaper, the *Dearborn [Michigan] Independent*, published a long series of articles defending the authenticity of the *Protocols*. These articles were published as a book, *The International Jew*, which Nazi leader Adolf Hitler later had translated and circulated throughout Germany.

The book encouraged readers to form a Franco-Russian league to combat the powers of the Jewish people. Rachkovsky attempted to create such a league in 1902; although he failed, he later succeeded in creating the Union of the Russian People. Founded in 1905, the union conducted anti-Jewish activities, which included helping to circulate the *Protocols*.

In 1902, Rachkovsky was involved in a court intrigue with Sergey Nilus in St. Petersburg, Russia. A former

PROPAGANDA:

The spreading of ideas, information, or rumor for the purpose of helping or injuring an institution, a cause, or a person. (*Webster's Ninth*)

Translations of the *Protocols* began to circulate in Europe around 1919. Publication in Germany began in 1920 (although the earliest title page is dated 1919); sales quickly reached 120,000 copies. The 1922 assassination of German Foreign Minister Walther Rathenau was motivated by the idea that Rathenau, a Jew, was one of the "Elders of Zion."

An English translation, called *The Jewish Peril*, was published in 1920 by Eyre & Spottiswoode, publishers of the authorized version of the Bible and Anglican Prayer Book. Most reviewers accepted the work as authentic, although the newspapers published letters from readers who disagreed.

GENOCIDE:

The deliberate and systematic destruction of a racial, political, or cultural group (*Webster's Ninth*)

landowner, Nilus had lost his entire fortune while living in France. After wandering in Russia from one monastery to another, he published a book in 1900. Nilus's book, *The Great in the Small*, explained how he had converted from an atheist to an Orthodox Christian.

"Evidence" of a worldwide conspiracy. Somehow, Nilus obtained a copy of the *Protocols*; many believe that Rachkovsky sent him a copy, perhaps to continue their St. Petersburg court intrigue. When Nilus published a second edition of *The Great in the Small* in 1905, he included the *Protocols* as documentary "evidence" of a worldwide Jewish conspiracy. It seems Nilus believed that the world was in the throes of a Jewish takeover.

Once Nilus's version of the *Protocols* was published in 1905, the work took on a life of its own. Czar Nicholas II read and accepted the *Protocols*—which had been widely circulated in right-wing circles in Russia—as genuine. Once an investigation demonstrated that the work was a fraud, however, Nicholas refused to continue to allow the *Protocols* to be used as anti-Semitic propaganda.

The situation changed when the Czar was overthrown in the Russian Revolution. The "White" army, which had lost to the "Red" army, blamed the revolution on the Jews. The *Protocols* was widely read by the members of the "White" army, who believed that the work explained why and how the Jews were attempting to take over the world. This was the beginning of the myth of the Jewish-Communist conspiracy that helped to fuel the German campaign of anti-Semitism.

German nationalists and the "Jewish World Conspiracy." Beginning in 1920, the German National People's Party (DNVP) used racist propaganda—including the *Protocols*—in election campaigns. These campaigns focused on the "Jewish World Conspiracy"—a Jewish plot to destroy the "Aryan," or Germanic race. Fueled by the German nationalist tradition (the "volkisch-racist"), the *Protocols* reinforced the kind of attitudes that led to the Holocaust, where millions of people were killed.

The *Protocols* become a Nazi tool. Alfred Rosenberg, a writer who promoted Nazi anti-Semitism, was apparently influenced by the *Protocols* when he wrote *Myth of the Twentieth Century*, a book that came to be known as the sourcebook of Nazism. Hitler looked to the *Protocols*

Nazi leader Adolf Hitler believed the *Protocols of the Elders of Zion* to be part of a Jewish conspiracy to destroy the Aryan race.

for an explanation of the tremendous economic inflation of 1923: "According to the *Protocols of Zion*," Hitler claimed, "the peoples are to be reduced to submission by hunger. The second revolution under the Star of David is the aim of the Jews in our time."

The *Protocols*, which had started out as a hoax, probably for Russian political reasons, thus became a deadly justification of anti-Semitism. Later referred to as a "warrant for genocide," the *Protocols of the Elders of Zion* was probably the most lethal hoax ever conceived.

Tales From the Other Side

A SHARP MEMORY

It has been demonstrated that a person can remember foreign languages heard in childhood—even without understanding the language. An individual can repeat perfect sentences even though he or she does not consciously remember hearing or speaking the language before. The mind can also remember historical facts that have been lost to the conscious memory.

BRIDEY MURPHY AND PAST LIVES

The Search for Bridey Murphy, by Morey Bernstein, was a best-seller in 1956. Bernstein, an amateur hypnotist, uncovered Bridey Murphy, an Irish woman from the early nineteenth century, quite by accident. Using hypnosis, he "regressed" a woman he called Ruth Simmons backwards in time; so far back in time, in fact, she remembered a previous life.

Nineteenth-Century Irish Woman Returns to World of Living!

The Bridey Murphy case was hardly the first time that a person had been regressed past birth under hypnosis. But, publicity, in the form of newspaper coverage and a best-selling novel, set this story apart from the others. The public was quick to believe a tale that suggested it was possible to survive death. When *Denver Post* reporter William J. Barker wrote several articles about the story for his newspaper's Sunday magazine section, Bridey Murphy took her place in history.

Doubleday, a large publishing company, eventually offered Bernstein a book contract, and the story of Bridey Murphy hit the best-seller list. At the same time, the *Chicago Daily News* obtained the rights to republish parts of the book; this inspired the paper's arch rival, the *Chicago American*, to assign reporters to look for holes in the story. After discovering that Ruth Simmons—whose real name was Virginia Tighe—had spent much of her youth in Chicago, Illinois, the investigators came

across a number of interesting details about the woman who had been hypnotized in Pueblo, Colorado.

Memories of a past life. When Bernstein asked Virginia Tighe to remember what had happened to her before birth, she volunteered a wealth of memories. This was the story of Bridey Murphy: Born in 1798 in Cork, Ireland, Bridget (Bridey) Kathleen Murphy was the daughter of Kathleen and Duncan Murphy, a Protestant barrister (lawyer). Bridey lived with her family, which included a brother, Duncan Blaine Murphy, just outside of Cork, in an area she called "The Meadows." Under hypnosis, Bridey remembered being punished for scratching the paint off of her metal bed when she was about four years old; she also remembered being read to as a child from two books, *The Green Bay* and another about the sorrow of Dierdre.

At the age of twenty, Bridey married Sean Brian Joseph MacCarthy, the son of another Cork barrister. Since MacCarthy's family was Catho-

lic, they had two wedding ceremonies, one Protestant and one Catholic, performed by Father Joseph John Gorman at St. Theresa's Church in Belfast. Bridey and Sean made their home in a cottage on Dooley Road in Belfast.

Bridey's brother married Aimee Strayne, the daughter of Bridey's school mistress. The couple stayed in Cork and had children; Bridey and her husband, on the other hand, had no children. Sean, a barrister who taught at the law school at Queen's University in Belfast, also wrote about the law in the *Belfast News-Letter*. Bridey died in 1864 at the age of sixty-six.

The facts are investigated. Some of the facts in Tighe's story could be proved—or disproved. The *Denver Post* sent William Barker over to Ireland for three weeks to check out the story. Barker—who was not an experienced genealogist and had little experience with historical research—found little to contradict Bridey's story. He didn't find much to support her story, either. What Barker did not realize was that Bridey's story was weakened by the fact that he did not find her husband's name on the lists of barristers: The lists at that time were both complete and accurate. Barker nonetheless had an idea why Bridey's husband's name was absent from the lists: Bridey exaggerated and had probably "remembered" a more glamorous profession for her bookkeeper husband.

***Life* calls Bridey's story "Hypnotizzy."** The *Chicago American*'s investigators were not so inclined to believe that Virginia Tighe was remembering her 100-year-old past. Tighe, it turns out, had an aunt who was born in Ireland. As a child in Chicago, she had listened to her aunt's many stories of her own childhood in the land of Erin. Across the street from young Virginia lived another Irish woman, who also told her stories about Ireland; the woman's name was Bridie Murphy Corkell. *Life* magazine soon got wind of these findings, and published the news as the "solution" to the Bridey Murphy mystery.

William Barker responded to statements made by the *Chicago American* and *Life* by adding a chapter to the paperback edition of Bernstein's book. In it, he described some findings that supported Bridey's story. For example, Virginia Tighe had mentioned the names of two grocers, Carrigan and Farr; it's very difficult to explain how a woman who grew up in Chicago in the twentieth century would have known the names of two relatively unknown grocers who conducted business in Belfast for a few years in the mid-1800s.

Borrowed memories. Was Virginia Tighe the reincarnation of a nineteenth-century Irish woman, or was Bridey Murphy the woman who

FLAWS IN VIRGINIA TIGHE'S STORY

Tighe claimed to remember her life as a nineteenth-century Irish woman, yet there were some gaping holes in her memory.

1. She was unable to speak any Gaelic;

2. She could not remember where she was buried, although she said she had witnessed her own funeral;

3. She was unable to offer information that fit with atlases and directories of the time. Publications showed no St. Theresa's Church, Dooley Road, or Mrs. Strayne's Day School. There is no evidence of a MacCarthy family of barristers or of a Father Joseph John Gorman. There is no indication that there were metal beds in Ireland in 1802, and no one has located a book from that time called *The Green Bay*.

never was? It's possible that Tighe's memory was playing tricks on her: Bridey's "recollections" may be nothing more than Tighe's forgotten memories of childhood stories. The entire episode might be a case of a hypnotized person trying to please the hypnotist. Or Bridey Murphy might have crossed the Atlantic—and then some—to pay the world a second visit.

HARRY HOUDINI ATTEMPTS TO COMMUNICATE WITH THE DEAD

Ehrich Weiss, born in 1874, was better known as the celebrated magician Harry Houdini. Close to his mother, he was shaken when she died in 1913. He decided to find out whether there was any truth to the idea that the spirit of his dead mother could communicate with him through a spiritualist medium—a go-between who claims to have the power to contact spirits. It didn't take long for Houdini, an expert on magic and sleight of hand, to find that mediumship was full of fakery.

Houdini Breaks Silence of Grave!

A number of mediums attempted to convince Houdini that his mother's spirit was talking to him. What they didn't realize was that Houdini's mother spoke no English and always called him "Ehrich." Angered by his discovery that mediums preyed on a public that did not easily see through magic tricks, Houdini began a crusade to challenge and expose bogus mediums. As a result, people began to regard mediums with suspicion.

Magician plans his escape from the spirit world. Despite his disappointment in trying to contact the spirit of his mother, Houdini wasn't going to rule out the possibility of communicating with the living after he died. He arranged with his wife Bess to use a code that would show he was trying to contact her. The code was based on a stage magic act they had performed together, and there was little chance of anyone else knowing the routine at the time of Houdini's unexpected death on Halloween in 1926.

For several years, Bess Houdini attended seances on the anniversary of her husband's death. That she promised $10,000 to any who provided the correct message generated much interest, but none of the medium's messages employed the secret code that Houdini had worked out before he died.

A message from beyond. Three years after Houdini's death, Arthur Ford, a medium who was the pastor of the First Spiritualist Church of

New York City, told his congregation that Houdini's mother was trying to make contact. "Forgive," Ford claimed, was the message Houdini's mother wanted to relay to Bess. When Ford contacted her, Bess confirmed that "forgive" was indeed the secret message Houdini had planned to communicate from the spirit world. But Ford committed a telling mistake: He, too, claimed that Houdini's mother had called her son "Harry."

Ford's representatives, it turns out, had already met with Bess Houdini. Suffering from both a high fever and a concussion, she was in a semi-delirious state when Ford's people visited her in the hospital; it is quite possible that Bess could have imparted the "secret" message while in this mentally hazy state. Adding to the possibility that Ford picked up on the "secret" word is the fact that the word had been published about a year earlier in the *Brooklyn* [New York] *Eagle* newspaper.

Houdini's believe it or not. A few days after conveying the "message," Ford staged a seance in Bess Houdini's home. While supposedly in a trance, he repeated the entire coded part of the message. "Rosabelle, answer, tell, pray, answer, look, tell, answer, answer, tell"—Houdini's code for the word "believe"—seemed to be the spirit of the magician urging his wife (whose nickname was Rosabelle) to believe Ford's message.

While Bess believed that only she and Houdini knew the code, a magician by the name of Joseph Dunninger said otherwise: The code had been published on page 105 of Harold Kellock's biography of the magician, *Houdini: His Life Story*. Much of Houdini's life, in fact, was an open book: "Rosabelle," Houdini's pet name for his wife, was engraved on the back of her wedding ring, which she had shown to many people.

Failure to communicate. While in the hospital, Bess Houdini told reporters that there were three messages from Houdini locked in her safe deposit box; these were copies of messages that Houdini was supposed to send from the spirit world. Bess was to receive one message, Remigius Weiss was to receive another, and Arthur Conan Doyle (the author of Sherlock Holmes stories) was to receive the third. Both men denied that Houdini had promised them a message from the spirit world. Although Bess had promised to reveal the messages, she never did, and her attorney claimed there were no messages in her safe deposit box.

Bess later claimed that she did not know what the exact message from Houdini was to be: She knew only that it was to be a ten-word message given in the magician's secret code. Although Ford eventually admitted to a reporter that he had obtained the code from Houdini's wife, Bess denied it and repeatedly stated that no one had yet produced her husband's message. The master magician, it seems, did not manage to escape from the spirit world. But he did manage to prove himself right: Anyone can talk to the dead, but the dead don't answer.

THE LEVITATION OF DANIEL DUNGLAS HOME

Daniel Dunglas Home, who lived from 1833 to 1886, was perhaps the most famous physical medium who ever lived. Because he never charged for his seances—although he did accept gifts and hospitality—few of his "victims" were eager to expose him.

Man Floats In and Out of Windows Eighty Feet Above Ground!

Home frequently levitated. Witnesses said he seemed to float toward the ceiling in a semi-dark room. No one, however, actually saw

Home levitate: Most people assumed he had risen because they felt his feet near their faces.

Home was occasionally involved in spiritualistic frauds. He was caught, for example, taking his foot out of his shoe during a seance. The dimly lit atmosphere of the seance allowed Home to create the illusion of floating above his seated guests. Having secretly placed his shoes on his hands, he waved his shoe-clad hands in the air to give his guests the impression that his feet were at eye-level. Participants also reported that his voice came from high up—an effect Home could accomplish simply by standing on a chair before opening his mouth to speak.

Home's most fearful feat. What was probably Home's most famous levitation took place in the presence of Lord Adare, Lord Lindsay, and Captain Charles Wynne in December 1868. Adare described what happened that day in his book *Experiences in Spiritualism with D. D. Home.* The spiritualist went into a trance, walked around the room, went into the next room, and opened the window. Lindsay, who thought he knew what was about to take place, cried out that what was happening was "too fearful ... He is going out of the window in the other room and coming in at this window." (Lindsay later claimed he knew this through telepathic communication.) At this point, Home appeared at the outside of the window, opened it, and entered the room.

He then asked Adare to close the window in the other room. When Adare found the window open only eighteen inches, he expressed his amazement that Home *could* have passed through such a narrow opening. Home responded by showing him how he had managed: He shot through the window head first and returned the same way.

The story of Home's levitation is usually reported in this manner, sometimes embroidered with additional details. The windows, for example, were said to be eighty dizzying feet above ground, and they were separated by a seven-foot span with only a four-inch-wide ledge between them. Adding to the difficulty of slipping in and out of the windows at eighty feet above ground level was the fact that each window was encased by a wrought iron balcony.

FLOATING TABLES

Home also performed table levitations. Reports of his seances indicate that the table rose, uniformly, when people were seated around it joining hands on the table top. The table would then begin to rise, forcing whoever was seated to rise in order to maintain the circle of joined hands.

Home's levitating table might have been a trick, but it was no new trick. Fraudulent mediums had a history of using a device that consisted of a flat metal blade and straps that could be fastened to the arm under clothing. Two people on opposite sides of the table could engage the blades under the table top. Once the participants in the seance had placed their hands on the table, the two accomplices could announce that the table was rising. When they stood up, the table lifted with them—even though the circle of hands was unbroken—creating the illusion that the table was levitating.

Home stated that during levitation, he experienced a swollen and tingling sensation in his feet. He was usually lifted in an upright position, and his arms became rigid and drawn above his head as if he were grasping at some unseen power that was lifting him up from the floor. The spiritualist claimed to have remained levitated for as long as four to five minutes.

The details don't add up. Parts of Home's story just don't make sense. The date and location of the levitation have been misstated. Although Adare reports that the light from outside the window was bright, there was a new moon—and therefore little light—on the actual night of the levitation.

Saints, Spirits, and Supernatural Scams

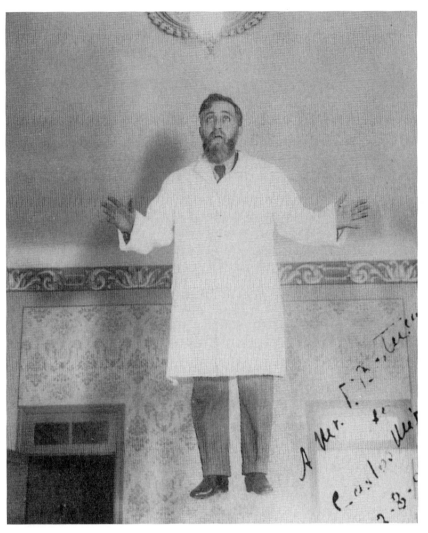

Mirabelli Floats!
(See page 56.)

And then there are the photographs of the building, which is no longer standing. They show two windows with balconies—only thirty-five feet above the ground—separated by what appears to be a mere four feet.

There are two details that make Home's levitation look even more suspicious. He consistently said that he had no control over his levitations, yet he told Adare and Lindsay that he was going out one window and in the other—a dangerous feat for someone aimlessly floating eighty feet above ground.

Home *could* have faked the window trick. If so, *how* did he do it? The "levitator" had plenty of time alone in the building and could have

AMERICAN LEVITATION

Home himself admitted that only one of his levitations occurred in daylight—in Connecticut, at the home of Ward Cheney in August 1852. Yet, F. L. Burr, who reported this levitation, says that it occurred in "a darkened room." Why would Home mistakenly claim that the levitation had taken place in daylight? Perhaps he confused this levitation with another; or perhaps he wanted to keep nonbelievers in the dark.

practiced jumping from one balcony to the other. Or he might have created an illusion under the cover of darkness: After opening the window in one room he could have slipped out of the room to open the other window. Standing on the *inside* ledge of the second window in the dark, he might have fooled a gullible witness into believing that he was actually standing outside the open window. The eyes can be deceived in the dark, especially under power of suggestion.

Mirabelli Floats. The only known photograph of a person actually levitating was the 1935 photo of the Brazilian medium Carlos Mirabelli (see page 55). Clad in a white lab coat, Mirabelli appeared to be rising to about six feet in the air with his arms lifted at his sides.

The Brazilian medium's secret? A stepladder. The original print, recently discovered, shows Mirabelli standing on the top step of a ladder. The ladder was clumsily airbrushed out of copies of the photo, and the alterations were concealed by the flowered pattern of the wallpaper in the room.

PARAPSYCHOLOGY:

A field of study concerned with finding and investigating evidence of unusual psychological experiences, such as extrasensory perception (ESP), clairvoyance (the ability to perceive matters that are beyond the range of ordinary perception), and psychokinesis (the movement of physical objects by the mind).

THE SOAL AND LEVY HOAXES

Dr. S. G. Soal and Dr. Walter J. Levy were parapsychologists. Both performed experiments that seemed to provide impressive documentation of the existence of extrasensory perception (ESP).

Scientists Document Proof of ESP!

As a recent graduate of medical school, Levy was drawn to parapsychology rather than medicine. He moved to Durham, North Carolina, to join the Institute for Parapsychology, where he conducted a number of studies involving paranormal happenings. The director of the institute, Dr. J. B. Rhine, was impressed by Levy's energy, and in 1973, he appointed Levy as the new director of the Institute of Parapsychology.

Rumors of false data. In 1973, rumors began to fly: Levy, his colleagues suspected, had misrepresented or falsified data. But there was no hard evidence, at least not until the summer of 1974, when Levy was seen "hanging around" the computer during an experiment. This was

odd since the equipment was fully automated and did not require Levy's attention during the experiment.

Suspecting foul play, laboratory workers decided to lay a trap for the institute's new director. By installing a second set of wires, they obtained a second set of data. If the results of both sets of data were not comparable, they would have evidence that Levy had tampered with the experiment. There was little doubt that Levy had a hand in tampering with the data: A hidden observer saw him manipulate the equipment so that the computer would register a string of "hits." The second set of data, on the other hand, showed only random scoring.

Levy confesses to fraud. When Rhine got wind of the lab workers' findings, he immediately con-

Levy authored twenty studies between 1969 and 1974. His research included investigating the clairvoyant abilities of mice to jump or run faster to avoid an electric shock that they knew was coming—although they did not know when or where the shock would come. He was also interested in finding out whether chicken embryos could use their minds (psychokinetically) to increase the amount of time a heat lamp, which supplied them with warmth, was turned on.

fronted Levy with the evidence. Levy confessed to fraud, but insisted that he had falsified only recent experiments. Blaming his lapse in ethics on being "overworked," he found little sympathy; Levy was fired shortly thereafter.

Researchers began to question all of Levy's previous research, and it soon became clear that fraud was a common theme in his studies. James Terry, who had worked with Levy on some of his early research, was alarmed by these developments. Terry called Rhine to urge him to repeat all the work he had done with Levy, and Rhine agreed—at least for the time.

Terry's first attempts to reproduce Levy's findings showed no significant evidence of ESP. Rhine refused to allow Terry to publish his results, nor did he allow the researcher to publish a whole series of results that failed to reproduce the positive results of Levy's experiments. Terry eventually went over Rhine's head; Charles Honorton, the president of the Parapsychological Association, allowed Terry to report his results at an association annual meeting.

Soal Searches for Signs of Extrasensory Perception (ESP)

By conducting card-guessing experiments, Dr. S. G. Soal set out to reproduce the results of J. B. Rhine's earlier work in ESP. Starting in 1934, Soal tested 160 people. Conducting 57,000 telepathy trials and 70,000 clairvoyance trials, he failed to show any significant presence of ESP. He did, however, discover some startling results: Participants seemed to "guess" a card correctly when it came immediately *before* or *after* the correct card to be guessed.

Soal analyzed the tests of a man named Basil Shackleton, whose scores indicated that he "hit" the target card only by chance. However, when Soal analyzed Shackleton's results for one card before or one card after the intended target, he discovered scores significantly *above* chance.

Soal retests two subjects. In 1940, Soal sought out Shackleton for further experiments. He also retested Gloria Stewart, a subject who had shown the same significant tendency to score above chance. Soal reported his results in 1943, and repeated them, in summary form, in 1954. In all, Soal had conducted some 12,000 trials with Shackleton and 50,000 trials with Stewart in this new set of experiments.

Witness claims Soal fudged data. Several years later, Gretl Albert, who had been present at some of the trials, reported that she had seen Soal alter some of the responses in ink while the experiment was being run. Soal denied the accusation. An examination of some of the score sheets—some of which were supposedly lost—revealed no obvious alterations. However, the numbers Soal had supposedly used to randomize the trials were analyzed by computer. The results did not match any table of random numbers that was tested. What's more, computer examination of other aspects of Soal's results showed more irregularities.

Clearly, Soal's data was manipulated. It is not known how it was done, or whether Soal consciously altered the data. It is known that Soal's card-guessing data offers no concrete proof of the existence of extrasensory perception.

SOAL'S EXPERIMENT

Soal's experiment consisted of five cards with a picture of an animal (such as a lion, elephant, giraffe, pelican, or zebra), placed face down in front of the subject. One number from one to five would be displayed, and the subject was asked to guess which animal was pictured on the card bearing that number.

Haunted Houses,
Cryptic Curses,
and Forecasts
of the
Faraway Future

Tall Tales of Doom and Gloom

THE HOUSE OF BLOOD

In the summer of 1987, a number of newspapers reported on a house in Atlanta that was oozing blood through the walls, ceilings, and floors. The blood was reportedly human.

It seems the story was blown out of proportion. Several squirts of blood—such as might be found if a single intravenous bag of blood were squeezed a few times—were found in several rooms of the house. The blood did not match the type of either of the elderly occupants of the house; it **probably** came from another member of the family who was undergoing kidney dialysis, and could have accidentally squirted blood from the vessel to which the dialysis tubing was connected. Satisfied by this explanation, the police pronounced the House of Blood to be a case closed.

THE AMITYVILLE HORROR

No one knows exactly what happened at the Dutch colonial house on Ocean Avenue in Amityville, New York, in 1975 and 1976. The best-selling—and supposedly nonfiction—book and movie about the haunting do little to resolve the Amityville mystery; as a matter of fact, they add to the confusion surrounding the supernatural story.

Haunted House Frightens Family of Five!

Few sources agree on the facts concerning the "Amityville Horror." What is known is this: On November 13, 1974, Ronald DeFeo killed six members of his family in the house on Ocean Avenue. Tried and convicted, he failed to convince the judge that he had obeyed voices that had told him to kill, and he was sentenced to six consecutive life terms.

The price was right. In November 1975, a realtor showed George and Kathy Lutz the house on Ocean Avenue. Although they had been informed of the colonial's grisly history, the price was right, and they decided to purchase the Amityville home.

On December 18—the day the Lutzes moved in with their three children—they supposedly had a priest bless the house. During his blessing, the priest is said to have heard a loud voice say "Get out!" Less

than one month later, the Lutzes moved out, leaving their possessions behind.

Money trouble. Even though George's business was not doing well, the Lutz family managed to finance the $80,000 Amityville home. In over his head with an unsound purchase, George soon realized that he could not continue to make his house payments. The Lutzes needed a way out of their financial troubles, and a haunted house looked like just the ticket.

Meanwhile, William Weber, the lawyer for murderer Ronald DeFeo, was trying to have his client cleared of murder charges by reason of insanity. When that didn't work, he planned to have DeFeo change his tune: "The devil made me do it" was to be the murderer's new line of defense.

It isn't clear who first came up with the idea of a haunted house on Ocean Avenue; there is little doubt, however, that the plan gradually evolved among the Lutzes, lawyer Weber, and Paul Hoffman, the first writer to publish anything about the creepy colonial.

Six bodies were found shot in the house on Ocean Avenue in Amityville, New York.

GREEN SLIME AND MYSTERIOUS MUSIC

The Lutzes later claimed that they had been tormented during their brief stay by a wide variety of supernatural events. They complained about:

- an infestation by hundreds of flies in the middle of winter
- moving statues
- green slime oozing from the ceiling
- a telephone that didn't work right
- a constant chill
- apparitions (ghostly figures)
- mysterious music

Amityville—the book. Jay Anson, a writer who had worked on the screenplay of *The Exorcist*, was brought in to tell the Amityville story. Although he was not allowed to enter the house and never even interviewed the Lutzes, he did have a series of tapes in which the family outlined their account of the horror on Ocean Avenue.

Anson got a bit carried away. Borrowing heavily from *The Exorcist,* he allowed his imagination to author the book. And he was careless about details: In his rush to complete the book, Anson wrote a story full of contradictions. The floor plan of the house, for example, changed several times in later printings of the book.

Anson's book is also chock full of outright falsehoods. Lutz admits that no one in his family ever saw the face of a pig. No marching band ever paraded through the house and no heavy door was torn off its hinges. No levitation occurred while Lutz was awake—although he admits that he might have dreamed it. The house was not built on a graveyard of the Shinnecock Indians. No windstorm or heavy snowstorm occurred on the nights that the book says they did. And no policeman was ever called to witness the cloven-foot tracks in the snow; in fact, there was no snow.

In a transcript of a trial that was held in September 1979 (*Lutz v. Hoffman*), the Lutzes admitted that almost everything in the book by Jay Anson was fiction. In fact, whenever the Lutzes, Anson, and Weber had to swear under oath about the so-called facts in the Anson book, no one could confirm any of the strange happenings as they are portrayed in *The Amityville Horror.*

The story of the Amityville horror couldn't be further from the truth. The fact is, the Lutzes—haunted by financial woes—became involved in a haunted house hoax for profit. And the supporting players in the scam did a superb job of selling the hoax to the public: Few people know that the whole episode was a hoax. Although the Amityville horror has been exposed as a fraud on a number of occasions, no exposure has ever rivaled the popularity of the book and movie that recount the fictitious haunting of the house on Ocean Avenue.

Family plagued by gawkers. Nothing out of the ordinary ever happened to the Cromartys, who moved into the house after the Lutzes abandoned it. The new owners did, however, sue the Lutzes because they were plagued by an onslaught of sightseers who stopped to check out the infamous address. The Lutzes settled out of court for an undisclosed amount.

THE HOPE DIAMOND CURSE

John Baptiste Tavernier brought the Hope Diamond—originally a 112.5 carat blue diamond—from India to France in the sixteenth century. Although he would not reveal where he found the diamond, it was rumored to have been stolen from the eye of a religious idol in a temple in Mandalay, Burma. Somewhere along the way, the diamond earned a reputation for being cursed: Anyone who owned the magnificent jewel would suffer an untimely death.

Spectacular Diamond Dooms Its Owners to Death and Devastation!

When Tavernier first brought the stone to France, it was purchased by the only man in France who could afford it—the Sun King, Louis XIV (who reigned from 1643 to 1715). Tavernier, whose business had failed, eventually died in Russia. Louis lived to old age and passed the 112.5-carat rock on to his descendants. When Louis XVI (who reigned from 1774 to 1792) inherited the diamond, he presented it to his wife, Marie Antoinette. Both suffered a bit a bad luck when they lost their heads—to the guillotine—in the French Reign of Terror.

A mysterious disappearance. The diamond disappeared, probably stolen during the French Revolution, and eventually surfaced in London, England, having shrunk to 44.5 carats in size—still a sizeable rock. No one knows what happened to the remainder of the diamond, which might have been cut into smaller fragments.

Hope purchases diamond. After banker Henry Hope bought the diamond (which now bears his name), he lived to a normal age without any noticeable ill effects from its "curse." When Hope died, the diamond was passed on to members of his family without causing any untimely deaths or spates of bad luck.

Only May Yohe, the wife of Lord Francis Hope, complained that the diamond brought her bad luck. The Hope family had sold the jewel in 1901, and in 1938, Yohe died in poverty due to bad investments.

POLTERGEISTS IN EIGHTEENTH-CENTURY ENGLAND

Poltergeist experiences often involve rapping sounds, thrown objects, broken dishes, and similar acts by "noisy spirits" (the German meaning of the word). Some people believe the weird goings-on to be ghostly pranks; others believe in more rational explanations.

In 1772 in Stockton, Surrey, England, there was an outbreak of strange happenings at the home of an elderly widow. Plates crashed from a shelf, an egg sailed across the kitchen (to break on a cat's head), and objects—such as a cask of beer in the cellar—were overturned. Later, a young maid who was suspected of causing the disturbances confessed to a clergyman that she had yanked a hidden wire to dislodge the plates, pelted the cat with the egg, and secretly performed the other acts attributed to mysterious forces.

A rare profile: New York jeweler Harry Winston—who never permitted photographers to capture him head-on—admires the 44.5-carat Hope Diamond.

The Hope Diamond.

Forty-four carat bad luck. After the Hope family sold the family jewel, hard times befell the rock's many owners. Of the next two owners—both of whom were jewelers—one went bankrupt and the other killed himself. The Russian nobleman who owned it next was stabbed to death by Russian revolutionaries. A Greek jeweler who owned it fell off a cliff, and the stone's Turkish owner—a sultan—was removed from his throne.

The jewel was eventually sold by Cartier's, an internationally famous jeweler, to Edward B. McLean, an American newspaper heir. More bad luck followed. McLean's only son was struck and killed by a car. His wife, Evalyn, divorced him and he was committed to a mental hospital where he died. Evalyn McLean continued to wear the diamond, even though ill fortune continued: In 1946, the McLeans' daughter committed suicide. The following year Evalyn McLean died at an advanced age.

New York jeweler Harry Winston bought the diamond and displayed it for several years before he donated it to the Smithsonian Institution in 1958. The diamond made the trip from New York to Washington, D.C., with little fanfare: Winston sent the gem—which was registered and insured for $1 million—through the regular mail, and the stone arrived safely.

A hoax, a curse, or just a lot of bad luck. Many of the diamond's owners—such as Louis XIV, Evalyn McLean, Henry Hope, and Harry Winston—did not die young. Others who owned the diamond briefly were unscathed by the experience. Although there is no arguing that a number of the diamond's owners did hit rock bottom, there's no solid connection between ownership of the Hope Diamond and early death. If there is a curse on the gemstone, it's slumbering safely in the Smithsonian.

THE CURSE OF KING TUTANKHAMEN

In 1922 Howard Carter discovered the tomb of Tutankhamen; what he found was one of the most magnificent treasures ever unearthed. Carter later described the moment of his astonishing find:

> Slowly, desperately slowly, it seemed to us, the remains of the passage debris that encumbered the lower part of the door was removed, until at last we had the whole door before us. The decisive moment had arrived. With trembling hands, I made a tiny breach in the upper left-hand corner ... Candle tests were applied to precaution against foul gases and then, widening the hole a little, I inserted the candle and peered in. At first I could see nothing, the hot air escaping from the chamber, causing the candle flame to flicker but presently, as my eyes grew accustomed to the light, details of the room within emerged slowly from the mist; strange animals, statues and gold—everywhere the glint of gold. For the moment I was struck dumb with amazement, and when Lord Carnarvon, unable to stand the suspense any longer, inquired anxiously, "Can you see anything?" it was all I could do to get the words, "Yes, wonderful things!"

Ancient Egyptian Boy King Curses All Who Enter His Sacred Tomb!

According to legend, anyone who entered the tomb of King Tutankhamen—best known as "King Tut"—soon died of an ancient curse that

BIG ROCKS

The value of a diamond is determined by demand, beauty, durability, rarity, freedom from defects, and perfection of cutting. The basic unit of weight is a carat, which is 200 milligrams; a well-cut round diamond of 1 carat measures almost exactly ¼ inch in diameter.

Even at its original size, the Hope Diamond would not be the world's largest stone. The Cullinan Diamond, discovered in 1905 in South Africa, weighed 3,106 carats before it was cut into nine major stones and ninety-six smaller gems. Cullinan I, also known at the "Greater Star of Africa" or the "First Star of Africa," is a pear-shaped diamond weighing 530.2 carats. Cullinan II, the "Second Star of Africa"—an oblong stone that weighs 317.4 carats—is set in the British Imperial State Crown.

According to legend, the boy king cursed all who entered his sacred resting place, including the officials who examined his mummy.

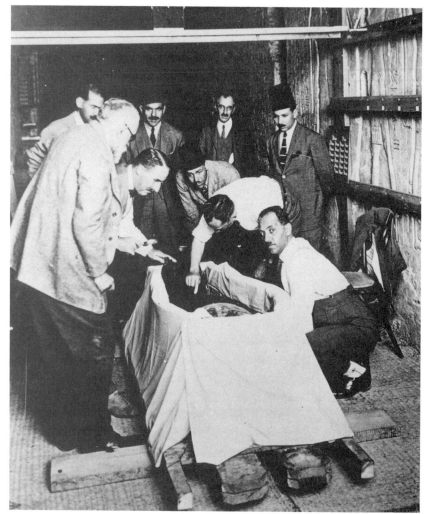

was inscribed as a warning at the entrance of the tomb. Today, nobody knows the whereabouts of the inscription, and it's possible that no one ever did. What's more, some of the people who first entered the tomb—including Howard Carter, the first to enter—lived many years after visiting the resting site of the ancient Egyptian king.

Scholars are not entirely sure who Tutankhamen was. He was probably the son of the infamous Akhenaten, who was king of Egypt for seventeen years (1379-1362 B.C.) during the Eighteenth Dynasty of the New Kingdom. His mother might have been Queen Kiya, one of Akhenaten's minor wives, who disappeared about the time that Tutankhamen was born in 1370. The young king (only nine years old) assumed the throne (after Akhenaten died) in 1361 and married the dead king's surviving daughter, Ankhesenpaaten. Tutankhamen ruled as king of Egypt until he died in 1352 at the age of eighteen. Today, the boy king known as King Tut is best remembered for the awesome treasure that was discovered inside his tomb.

It all started with a dead canary. It all began when Lord Carnarvon's pet canary died. The Lord, who sponsored an expedition to the tomb, died a little while later. At this point, a French Egyptologist and occultist, J. S. Mardus, stated in a Paris news conference that the tomb contained "all the things which the priests and masters of the funeral ceremony were able to place in the way of protection against profaners [violators]." He also suggested that other curses had protected other tombs in the past, and mentioned deaths at other tombs as evidence.

Although a number of other people reportedly involved with Tutankhamen's tomb *did* die within a few years of its opening, many who were involved did not die shortly thereafter.

Herbert E. Winlock, the director of the Metropolitan Museum of Art in New York, tallied the number of people who had been present at the 1922 opening of the tomb who had died by 1934. The results were hardly staggering: Of the twenty-two people who were present at the opening, only six had died. Of the separate group of twenty-two people who had witnessed the opening of the King's sarcophagus (stone coffin) in 1924, two died during the next decade. Ten people were present when the mummy was unwrapped in 1925, and all ten lived to tell about it in 1934.

The deaths of those who were present at the various openings were from natural causes. A few fell victim to diseases native to the area—not a startling fate for foreigners unaccustomed to local conditions.

Why did Egyptians make mummies? The ancient Egyptians who buried Tutankhamen believed in life after death. They believed that every living body is inhabited by a double, or *ka*, that does not necessarily die when the mortal body dies. They also believed that they could provide their departed loved ones with a more comfortable afterlife by constructing tombs, preserving the corpse through mummification, and furnishing goods and sustenance for the spirit double. The *ka*—a miniature image of the body—had to be fed, clothed, and served just as the living body had been.

The *ka* was supposed to have a better chance at eternity when the cadaver was protected against time and decay: Dead bodies were treated to prevent decomposition, and were buried in a sarcophagus. Herodotus,

King Tut's coffin.

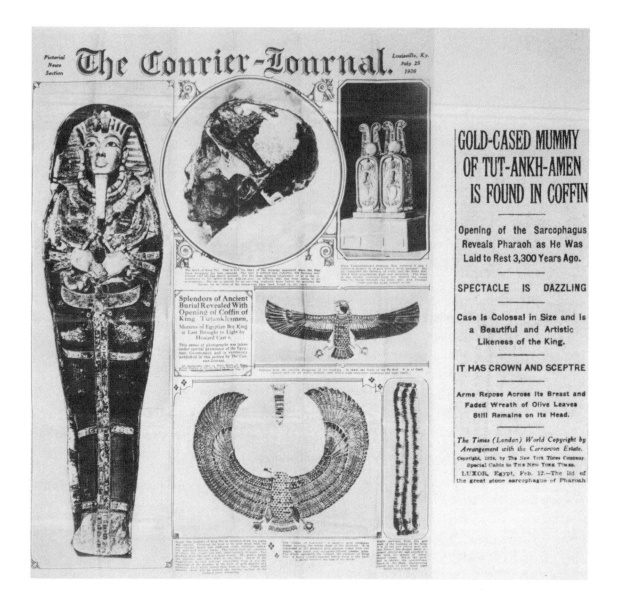

Newspapers around the world, like the Louisville, Kentucky, *Courier-Journal*, covered the opening of Tut's tomb.

an ancient Greek historian, provided a graphic description of the art of the embalmer:

> First they draw out the brains through the nostrils with an iron hook, raking part of it out in this manner, the rest by the infusion of drugs. Then with a sharp stone they make an incision in the side, and take out all the bowels; and having cleansed the abdomen and rinsed it with palm wine, they next sprinkle it with pounded perfume. Then, having filled the belly with pure myrrh, cassia and other perfumes, they sew it up again; and when they have done this they steep it in natron [a salt

derived from sodium and aluminum].... At the expiration of seventy days they wash the corpse, and wrap the whole body in bandages of waxen cloth, smearing it with gum, which the Egyptians commonly use instead of glue. After this the relations, having taken the body back again, make a wooden case in the shape of a man, and having made it they enclose the body; and then, having fastened it up, they store it in a sepulchral chamber, setting it upright against the wall. In this manner they prepare the bodies that are embalmed in the most expensive way.

The Pharaoh's curse. Reports that a curse was inscribed on the entrance of the tomb, or somewhere inside, were completely false: A carved or written curse was never found on or in the tomb. Yet somehow, the text of the curse fell into the hands of journalists eager to provide inquiring minds with the last word of the late King Tut.

NOSTRADAMUS'S PREDICTIONS

Michael Nostradamus (Michel de Notredame) was a French physician of probable Jewish ancestry who lived from 1503 to 1566. His prophetic work, *The Centuries*, predicted what would happen in the future, and was probably first published in 1555.

Sixteenth-Century Physician Predicts Outcome of World War II!

Today there are no known copies of Nostradamus's 1555 edition of *The Centuries*. The work was arranged in quatrains—four-line verses, each consisting of two rhymed pairs—and the book was written in a form of medieval French that was antiquated even when Nostradamus wrote it. The text was vague, and could easily be translated and interpreted in different ways.

Not all verses present in modern editions of the book date back to Nostradamus's time. Some editions contain 58 quatrains that were added sometime after the physician penned his predictions.

Nostradamus predicts the death of a king. What is probably the best-known quatrain supposedly predicted, in detail, the death of King Henry II of France, who lived from 1519 to 1559. It has been translated as follows:

THE LEGENDARY POWERS OF THE PYRAMIDS

The legendary powers of the pyramids have taken on the characteristics of a hoax. Originally, some people believed that the dimensions of the Great Pyramid (the Pyramid of Cheops) mirrored great mathematical relationships. From this came the idea that the structure of the pyramid itself formed some kind of coded message about the earth's future. This was all possible—according to some journalists—because the Great Pyramid was actually constructed by ancient alien astronauts.

Modern pyramid studies assert that placing a sharp object under a pyramid will preserve its sharpness, even with repeated use. They also claim that perishables such as fruit will not rot if they are placed under a pyramid, and that sleeping under a pyramid shape is somehow beneficial to one's health. None of these studies, however, produces reliable evidence to support the supposed miraculous effects of pyramid shapes.

MICHEL NOSTRADAMUS.
Médecin,
Né à S.ᵗRemy, en Provence, le 14 Décemb. 1503.
Mort le 2 Juillet 1566.

The young lion shall overcome the old
On the field of battle in single combat;
In a cage of gold he shall burst his eyes—
Two fleets one, then to die, a cruel death.

Although Henry II was killed when he was pierced through the eye
while jousting with a captain of his guard, few of the details of his death

match Nostradamus's predictions. The word "fleets" was later changed to "wounds," but Henry suffered only one wound. The forty-year-old king died when a splinter from the captain's lance penetrated his brain, not his eye (still other sources say the splinter pierced his throat). The lion was the emblem of neither Henry nor his guard, and Henry's helmet was not gold. In short, the verses were hardly prophetic.

Yet another quatrain predicted great things for Henry II: The French king was to be "chief of the world" and would enjoy the title of "Victor." Nostradamus made these predictions in 1558, but Henry claimed no such fame before meeting his grisly fate the following year.

Small-town prophecies. Nostradamus was only interested in predicting things that would happen in his local area in the next few years. In fact, most of the references in the *Centuries* refer to events and places in France in the sixteenth century.

For example, one of the verses begins, "PAV, NAY, LORON." Some people have taken the words to be an anagram (a word or phrase that is made by rearranging the letters of another word or phrase) for "Napoleon"; in truth, however, they are the names of three neighboring towns (Pau, Nay, and Oloron) in southwestern France.

Documents dating directly to Nostradamus's lifetime prove that many of his predictions were just plain wrong. In a document written in 1564 by Catherine (mother to King Charles IX and Francis II) to Conetable (Catherine's godfather), she refers to predictions that Nostradamus had just personally predicted for her. Conetable, the physician said, would live to be ninety, and so would Catherine's son, Charles; nevertheless, Conetable died at the age of seventy-seven and Charles died in 1574 at the tender age of twenty-four.

Nostradamus and the Nazis. In 1943 Karl Ernest Krafft, an astrologer for the Nazi party, wrote a small book called *Nostradamus Predicts the Course of the War (Nostradamus prophezeit den Kriegsverlauf)*. The book contains a great many "improvements" of the sixteenth-century verses and predicts that Germany would win World War II.

A number of verses supposedly predict Nazi leader Adolf Hitler's involvement in the war. Among them is verse II:24, which is correctly translated as follows:

> Beasts mad with hunger will swim across rivers,
> Most of the army will be against the Lower Danube.
> The great one will be dragged in an iron cage
> When the child brother will observe nothing.

By translating some of the medieval French words differently, some people discovered an entirely new meaning in the verse. They took the word "Hister"—an old name for a portion of the Danube River—to refer to Hitler, and they took "Germain"—a medieval French word for "brother"—as a reference to Germany. There is no way of telling what, exactly, Nostradamus meant although educated guesses say that the verse refers to the Turkish advances in Hungary that occurred during the mid-sixteenth century.

A prophet with a poor success rate. Nostradamus's other verses have been carefully examined, and there is no reason to believe that any of them were meant to apply to events beyond the mid-sixteenth century. As for the physician's predictions for his own century, he was usually wrong. But generations of forgers and hoaxers have made a famous person of a false prophet.

THE TAMARA RAND HOAX

Tamara Rand, a so-called psychic, claimed that she had predicted the March 30, 1981, assassination attempt on Ronald Reagan on a TV show in January of that year.

Psychic Predicts Assassination Attempt on President Reagan!

The KNTV show, *Dick Maurice and Company*, had aired in Las Vegas, Nevada, on January 6, 1981—more than two months before John Hinkley's attempt on President Reagan's life. The psychic predicted that she saw the president shot in the chest at the end of March or early April by a young, fair-haired man who acted alone. The young man would be from a wealthy family and would have the initials "J. H."

NBC's *Today* show and ABC's *Good Morning America* broadcast the tape on April 2, 1981. After carefully examining Rand's appearance, however, an Associated Press reporter discovered that the tape had actually been made in the Las Vegas studios of KNTV on March 31, one day *after* the shooting. Although Rand had, indeed, appeared on Dick Maurice's show in early January, she did not predict the attempt on Reagan's life at that time.

Talk show host helps psychic. With the assistance of Maurice, Rand attempted to restage her January appearance. Wearing the same dress, she tried to pass off her March "prediction" as part of the January segment of the television show.

Not everyone was convinced. An investigator noticed one dead giveaway: Rand wore different rings on her fingers on the "prediction" seg-

Psychic Tamara Rand on KNTV's *Dick Maurice and Company*. The interview was actually taped March 31, 1981, the day after the president was shot.

ment than she wore on the rest of the show. The microphones, too, were in slightly different positions.

When Maurice was confronted with this evidence, he admitted to the hoax—claiming it had been cooked up to boost the psychic's career—and was suspended from his show. Later, Rand also confessed.

The ABC and NBC networks, however, were not eager to admit that they had been scammed: It took a bit of prodding to convince them to retract their stories about the psychic's uncanny prediction. NBC later devoted an entire segment to the hoax, granting Rand's wish to become a celebrity psychic.

Globe-Trotting
and Gallivanting

Crafty Sailors and Sly Explorers

CHRISTOPHER COLUMBUS HOAXES

Explorer Christopher Columbus (1451–1506) was known for a number of things, but he wasn't known as a hoaxer. Yet a number of hoaxes have been committed in his name, long after he died. These include scams regarding the whereabouts of his remains and phoney writings penned by impostors.

Christopher Columbus's Bones Are Missing!

According to tradition, Columbus was buried in the cathedral of Santo Domingo, in the Dominican Republic. His remains were brought from Seville, Spain, in the 1540s, along with those of his son, Diego Columbus, at the request of Diego's widow, who lived in Santo Domingo.

The British attacked Santo Domingo in 1655, and the remains in the cathedral were concealed and forgotten. Some remains, however, were dug up in 1795 and taken to Havana, Cuba, where Columbus was to be memorialized. Although the identity of the remains was unknown, "tradition" identified the old bones as the remains of Columbus.

Father and son burial vaults. It seems that from the 1540s until 1795, there were two Columbus family vaults in the cathedral of Santo Domingo. One housed the body of Christopher Columbus, while the other contained the remains of his son, Diego. Apparently, Diego's remains, which had been buried on the other side of the church's presbytery, were exhumed and taken to Havana. In 1899, the remains were returned to Spain because Cuba had just been given to the United States when Spain lost the Spanish American War—Spain wanted Columbus's remains to stay in Spanish territory.

The hoax seems to have begun in 1795 when the Archbishop of Santo Domingo could not find the actual coffin of Christopher Colum-

Round and round the world he went, but where his bones are, nobody knows.

bus. He did, however, find Diego's coffin, which lacked a nameplate. Intentionally or unintentionally, the coffin was said to be that of Christopher Columbus.

In 1917, the two vaults were destroyed during the remodeling of the cathedral. One of them (Diego's) was thought to be empty, while the other, whose location was forgotten, contained the real remains of Christopher Columbus. Although Diego Columbus's remains were returned to the cathedral of Santo Domingo before going to Seville, the remains of Christopher Columbus have been lost. That means that any cathedral—including Santo Domingo—claiming to own the remains of Columbus is guilty of hoaxing the public.

Columbus's Only Writings

A more complex hoax involving Columbus has to do with a letter he wrote to his friend Luis de Sant Angel in 1493, describing his first voyage to the New World. In a letter that was supposed to be several pages long, Columbus told of the native peoples that he encountered. A printed version of this letter, which now resides in the archives of Simancas, Spain, is believed to have been published in 1493. At the same time, Columbus wrote another letter to his friend Gabriel Sanchez; the authenticity of this letter is not questioned. These two letters represent the only writings of Columbus.

References to the letter. The text of the de Sant Angel letter was first mentioned in 1825 in the *Colleccion de Viages* (published in Madrid), by Navarette, a nineteenth century Spanish travel writer. At first, it was believed to be the same as the Sanchez letter, several editions of which had been translated into Latin and published as early as 1493. Neither printed Spanish text lists a publisher, a place of printing, or a date of printing.

Although the contents of the two letters are similar, they were supposedly written separately and addressed to two different people. Some scholars believe that de Sant Angel had the text of his handwritten letter from Columbus printed in order to be able to reach a wider audience. Author Henry Harrisse, however, disagrees: After carefully examining the de Sant Angel letter, he concluded that it was a hoax, produced in the nineteenth century, probably based on the Sanchez letter.

The letter is sold and a lawsuit follows. In 1891, the copy that was used to produce a facsimile in 1889 (a London edition) was sold to an American for about $5,000—a very large sum at that time. The letter's new American owner eventually brought a law suit in a New York court on the grounds that he had been sold a forgery. A number of bibliographers (scholars who study the history and identification of writings) were brought in to testify. Few, however, had any real expertise in fifteenth century Spanish printing.

Someone pointed out that the spacing between the lines in the printed letter was irregular; how this could happen in set type—in which each letter is set evenly on a block of lead—was difficult to explain.

Additionally, the document included letters and letter forms that were not used in the 1490s.

Today, there are at least three different versions of the fake letter from Columbus to de Sant Angel. And no two letters are alike: Each letter has a different set of errors. It seems that by correcting the errors in previous letters, each forger introduced new errors. Author Henry Harrisse believes that Enrico Giordani of Milan was the original forger.

ROBERT PEARY AND THE NORTH POLE

On April 6, 1909, Admiral Robert E. Peary (1856–1920) claimed that he was the first person ever to reach the geographic North Pole. In spite of his questionable documentation, his claim was accepted, and Admiral Peary was hailed as a hero.

Explorer Lies About Reaching North Pole First!

A man by the name of Frederick A. Cook (1865–1940), however, did not regard Peary as a hero. Five days before Peary announced his success, Frederick Cook, who had been a surgeon on Peary's 1891 expedition, made his own announcement: He claimed that on April 21, 1908—nearly a year before Admiral Peary was supposed to have reached the North Pole—he had reached the site that had eluded so many other explorers. Mass confusion followed; two believable explorers were both claiming to be the first person ever to step foot on the northernmost point on earth.

A campaign to discredit Cook's and Peary's eye-opening records. Peary's supporters started a campaign to discredit Cook's claim, and the surgeon's life was deliberately ruined. Eventually, Cook was discredited and jailed for financial fraud.

The National Geographic Society was Peary's strongest supporter. The Society continued to defend him until 1988, when the evidence made it impossible to believe the admiral's story. Wally Herbert was hired to investigate, and bolster, Peary's claim; what he found was shocking. After examining the poorly documented records, Herbert concluded that Peary had not been the first man to reach the North Pole; in fact, Peary *never* reached the North Pole. Yet Herbert, who was still inclined to

THE Y'S HAVE IT

The de Sant Angel letter had one problem that was common to forgeries of early typesetting methods. Since each letter was set on a block of lead in fifteenth-century typesetting, individual letters could not take up any space of a preceding letter. That meant that the descending part of descending letters—such as the bottom part of the letters "j" and "y"—could not overlap letters (even if there were empty space below that letter).

But the descending letters in the de Sant Angel document did take up some of the space of preceding letters. That proves that the letter was not typeset, but was created by some photographic or artistic process. Since no such process was available in the 1490s, the de Sant Angel letter is, in a word, a fake.

Robert Peary and man's best friend.

believe the best of Peary, attributed the explorer's failure to document his expedition to incompetence rather than malice.

Author Dennis Rawlins then claimed to have found the records Peary made on the day he reached the Pole—records that Peary had said did not exist. Rawlins showed, by Peary's own calculations, that on April 6, 1909, Peary was 121 statute miles (or 105 nautical miles) short of the Pole. That was as far north as the arctic explorer ever ventured.

A secret in a safe deposit box. Peary apparently knew that he hadn't reached the North Pole. He gave his wife a document, saying that it was important and could destroy Frederick Cook's claim. Unable to understand the document, she placed the record in a safe deposit box.

Peary's calculations remained under lock and key until 1935, when his daughter sent a copy of the paper to Melville Grosvenor, the director of the American Geographical Society. The document forever

Much fur flew when Fred Cook fished for fame.

changed the way that people would remember Robert E. Peary: Fifteen years after the explorer died, Peary's daughter—who believed the paper supported her father's claim—had unwittingly exposed her father's fraud.

Harry Raymond, an astronomer, finally deciphered the document. It seems Peary's notations referred to sextant readings, which helped the explorer to navigate by measuring altitudes of celestial bodies. According to his own calculations, Admiral Peary was about 200 nautical miles from the North Pole at the time he claimed to have arrived there.

Even after the document was deciphered, it was sealed and its contents were not revealed. When Rawlins found the document again in 1973, he released the information that proved that Peary never set foot on the North Pole. Apparently, Peary was so inept at using his instruments that he never knew exactly where he was. But he must have known that he hadn't reached the North Pole: The sun does not rise and set in the sky at the Pole.

PEARY'S PREVIOUS
ATTEMPTS TO REACH
THE NORTH POLE

PEARY'S PREVIOUS ATTEMPTS TO REACH THE NORTH POLE

Robert Peary had led several previous attempts to reach the North Pole. After his first attempt (in 1891) failed, he tried an overland route through northern Greenland in 1892-1893. He failed again. Peary led another attempt in 1893-1895, and, in 1905-1906, he tried to reach the North Pole by ship. He failed yet again, although his last voyage did come within 174 miles of the Pole.

VIKINGS VISIT CANADA

L'Anse au Meadow in Newfoundland, Canada, contains the apparent remains of the only genuine Viking settlement in North America. The area is currently being explored.

VIKING HOAXES

Many people believe that the Vikings or other early visitors arrived in North America well before Columbus ever stepped foot on American soil. Evidence, however, is hard to find, and much of it can be easily dismissed. But two artifacts—the Vinland Map and the Kensington Runestone—were not quickly shelved: The yellowing old map and the characters carved in stone were just enough to convince some people that Viking voyagers had visited the New World.

Viking Explorers Beat Columbus to New World!

The Vinland Map, named after a territory in the New World, was found bound into a volume with two other manuscripts; one dated from the fifteenth century, while the other dated to the thirteenth century. There was no question that the map had been in the bound volume for some time since worm holes in the manuscript pages matched those in the map.

The map is drawn on a single piece of vellum—a fine-grained skin prepared for writing—and measures about eleven by sixteen inches, folded down the center. Drawn in ink, the map depicts the three known parts of the medieval world—Africa, Asia, and Europe. It was based on the kind of circular or oval style that was popular until the second half of the fifteenth century, and the names on the map are in Latin.

The most striking feature of the layout is the depiction of two large islands in the upper left corner of the map. One, called Gronelada, is clearly Greenland. The other one, further west and labeled "Vinlanda Insula," is what led some to believe they had found evidence that Vikings (or others) had traveled to the New World before Columbus. If this map had been drawn before Columbus was born, it must have relied on the "discoveries" of other explorers who came *before* Columbus.

A look under the microscope. A number of map experts have argued that the names, the wormholes, and the style of the map all suggest that it is an authentic Viking map. Nevertheless, Yale University, which acquired the map in 1957, decided to have the map tested. In

1972, McCrone Associates of Chicago—a firm that specializes in scientific testing of suspected art and other forgeries—carried out an investigation of the map.

To begin with, the contents of the map were suspect. McCrone Associates noted that although the map depicts Greenland and its coastline accurately, it is highly unlikely that a fifteenth-century mapmaker would have had such knowledge.

The firm also conducted microscopical and chemical investigations of the map. The microscopical examination revealed that the ink line that formed the outline of the countries was bordered along its length by a yellowish discoloration.

At first, this was attributed to the tendency for old ink to become discolored along its edges because parts of it have leaked into the fibers of the paper. But further examination produced another explanation for the yellowish marks: The discoloration on the map had a "body" of its own, and pieces of the "yellow" could be flecked from the line with a fine needle. Apparently, the black ink line had been drawn over a slightly wider yellow line that had been laid down first. In fact, in one spot, the black line had been carelessly drawn so that it did not match the yellow line.

Man-made pigment. Still other tests—with higher magnification and polarized light—showed particles of what turned out to be anatase in the yellow "ink." Anatase is a mineral, but the small and regular size of the anatase particles indicated that these were of a man-made variety. Anatase is a titanium white pigment that was not available before 1917.

The ink in the two manuscripts that were bound with the Vinland Map was also tested. The levels of titanium (of a natural sort) in these inks were much lower. In fact, they matched the levels found in real aged-iron gallate inks that were used at the time the map was supposed to have been composed.

In short, the two manuscripts really are genuinely old. The Vinland Map, on the other hand, couldn't have been drawn before 1917. The forgers, it seems, made only one serious mistake: They used a yellow ink that was too modern for the 1400s.

THE ROUND TOWER AT NEWPORT, RHODE ISLAND

Some people believe that the Round Tower at Newport, a haphazard fieldstone masonry structure, to be of Viking origins. In 1948 and 1949, William S. Godfrey, Jr., an amateur archaeologist, excavated the entire area around the tower. He found a number of artifacts, but they weren't from the Viking era. Rather, he discovered all sorts of colonial artifacts—such as clay pipes, glass fragments, ceramic shards, and a gun flint—**under** the stone foundations that support the tower.

Gun flints did not come along until well after the Viking era, yet they were found **beneath** the supposed Viking structure. That rules out any possibility that they were constructed before Columbus was born. In fact, the "Viking" tower was surely built during the American colonial period, probably in the 1650s.

A WEALTH OF VIKING ARTIFACTS

There are a great many supposed Viking artifacts from North America, including spears, axes, and swords. The axes are almost all socket-paring axes, a form of lumbering tool that has extra weight added to the butt for balance. Since this is strictly an American innovation, these axes can't possibly be of Viking origin.

The small halberds (tobacco-cutting swords), which have been discovered in many places, were not used in Scandinavia until after 1500. These swords are in fact plug tobacco cutters, made in the nineteenth century in Ohio. Although several genuine Norse weapons of great antiquity were found in Canada, it was later shown that they were brought there from Norway in the early twentieth century.

The Kensington Runestone— Runes Written in Stone!

The Kensington Runestone was a piece of flat sandstone about six inches thick, thirty inches long, and fifteen inches wide. It was found in 1898 by farmer Olof Ohman, on his farm in Kensington, Minnesota. Entangled in the roots of a tree no more than thirty years old, the stone was covered on one side with what appeared to be sharply cut rune—the writing of the ancient Scandinavians. The writing, which has been translated by several experts in Norwegian language, is as follows:

> Eight Goths and 22 Norwegians on an exploration journey from Vinland to the west. We had camp by 2 skerries one day's journey north from this stone. We were to fish one day after we came home found 10 men red of blood and dead AVM [Ave Maria]. We have 10 men by the sea to look after our ships 14 days' travel from this island Year 1362.

An ancient message in modern Swedish. Professor G.O. Curme, an expert in Germanic languages at Northwestern University, examined the stone. He remarked that it was odd that the stone, which dated itself to 1362, was written in modern Swedish with recent runes. He also noted that the cuts that formed the runes did not look old. With that, the stone was returned to Ohman.

Nine years later, a book salesman named Hjalmar Holand rediscovered the stone and spent the rest of his life advertising that it was an authentic Viking relic. His evidence, however, was less than reliable: He misquoted his sources, which were not readily available to those who listened to his defense of the stone. The experts were not impressed. After all, according to Norwegian language expert Professor Erik Wahlgren, the Swedish on the stone was a version of that language that had never been spoken anywhere outside the American Midwest.

A self-educated hoaxer. It looks like Ohman, a self-educated man, carved the stone himself. In fact, it even appears that his own speech peculiarities—reflected in his Halsingland dialect—were also present in the Runestone. He might have been helped by Sven Fogelblad, a former minister in Sweden, turned teacher, who knew runes well.

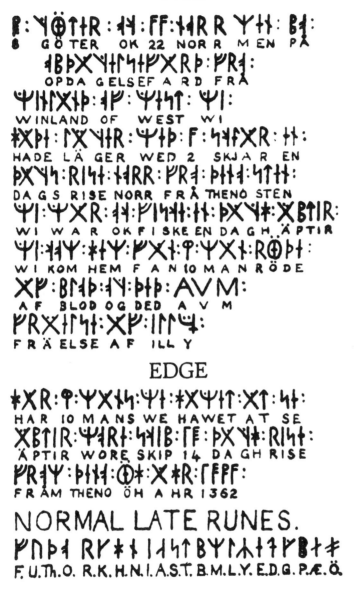

FACE

8 GÖTER OK 22 NORR MEN PÅ

OPDA GELSEFARD FRÅ

WINLAND OF WEST WI

HADE LÄGER WED 2 SKJAR EN

DAGS RISE NORR FRÅ THENO STEN

WI WAR OK FISKE EN DAGH ÄPTIR

WI KOM HEM FAN 10 MAN RÖDE

AF BLOD OG DED AVM

FRÄELSE AF ILLY

EDGE

HAR 10 MANS WE HAWET AT SE

ÄPTIR WORE SKIP 14 DAGH RISE

FRÅM THENO ÖH AHR 1362

NORMAL LATE RUNES.

F.U.Th.O. R.K.H.N.I.A.S.T. B.M.L.Y. E.D.G. P.Æ.Ö.

Ohman finally admitted that he knew how to read and write modern runes; he even had several books that illustrated runes. What's more, the Minnesota farmer was originally trained as a *stone mason*—a handy skill for a latter-day Viking.

Military
Maneuvers

Slick Soldiers and Slippery Spymasters

H.M.S. *DREADNOUGHT*

In 1910, England was very proud of its navy. The Channel Fleet—also known as the Home Fleet—was assembled for review at Weymouth, a port on the English Channel. The admiral of the fleet, Sir William May, was on the flagship *Dreadnought*. Soon, Horace de Vere Cole, a prominent prankster, would join him on board as part of a royal party of hoaxers.

Phoney Ethiopian Royalty Fool British Flagship and Fleet!

One February morning in 1910, de Vere Cole and his cohorts went—in full costume—to Paddington Station in London to catch a train to Weymouth. When the stationmaster was informed that members of the Ethiopian royalty were among the passengers at the London station, he arranged an impromptu reception for them on the platform.

While the group of hoaxers was on the train bound for Weymouth, another prankster (who has never been identified) sent a telegram to the admiral of the Channel fleet. Signed by the head of the British Foreign Office, the telegram informed Admiral Sir William May that a royal party was en route to Weymouth, and requested that he "kindly make all arrangements to receive them." This was news to the real head of the British Foreign Office, who did not learn of the forgery until days later.

When the "royal" party reached Weymouth, they were greeted with a red carpet welcome, complete with escort and car. After visiting a

---

THE CAST OF CHARACTERS

Prankster Horace de Vere Cole enlisted the cooperation of a number of other hoaxers. Naturalist Anthony Buxton, artist Duncan Grant, brother and sister Adrian and Virginia Stephen (who was later known as the famous author Virginia Woolf), and Guy Ridley, the son of a judge, all answered the casting call for the *Dreadnought* hoax. Four of the pranksters, made up in blackface and dressed in Ethiopian robes, became members of the Ethiopian royalty. Buxton portrayed the emperor, while Cole, dressed in top hat and tails, played Herbert Cholmondley of the Foreign Office.

The *Dreadnought* hoaxers.

Dreadnought special launch in the harbor, they were taken to the flagship where the party met the admiral, inspected a marine guard, and toured the ship.

As a light rain began to fall, disaster seemed inevitable: The blackface makeup and fake mustaches would not withstand the February showers. Fortunately, when someone suggested to the captain that everyone would be more comfortable inside, he agreed.

Picky eaters and rented costumes. Once back on shore, the Ethiopians boarded another train. De Vere Cole—as Herbert Cholmondley of the Foreign Office—told the railroad personnel that the Ethiopian visitors would not eat unless they were served by people wearing white gloves. When the train stopped at Reading, several people rushed out to find a store that sold white gloves, and the Ethiopian party was later served by waiters in proper attire.

Once back in London, the Ethiopians paused for a group photograph, washed off their blackface makeup, and returned their rented costumes. Unable to keep the hoax secret, de Vere Cole went to the London newspapers with his outrageous story. The group photograph and the story of the hoax appeared in several newspapers. Although none of the names of the hoaxers were used, they were revealed in 1936 when Adrian Stephen's *The "Dreadnought Hoax"* was published.

AND THE BAND PLAYED ON

When the Ethiopian party left the ship, the band struck up a rousing rendition of the national anthem of Zanzibar, which was at the time a British protectorate located considerably to the south of Ethiopia. The band, it seems, had been unable to find the music for the Ethiopian national anthem.

Stephen's book prompted a number of groups, including Scotland Yard and the Admiralty, to consider launching an investigation. But since the pranksters were guilty of nothing more serious than sending a forged telegram, the investigations were dropped.

JOHN PAUL JONES AND THE AMERICAN NAVY

John Paul Jones, a Scottish-born sailor who lived from 1717 to 1792, is usually given credit for founding the United States Navy. But credit—of some sort—belongs to Augustus C. Buell, the Jones biographer who made up the whole story.

John Paul Jones Wasn't Who People Thought He Was!

John Paul Jones, born simply John Paul, was drawn to the sea at an early age, becoming an apprentice seaman at the age of twelve. When he brought a merchant ship into port safely—after both the captain and the first mate had died—he was awarded 10 percent of the value of the cargo, and was given command of the ship.

After a difficult period as a captain, John Paul found himself in America, unemployed, at the beginning of the Revolutionary War. Having added "Jones" as his new last name, he obtained a position as an officer aboard the *Alfred*—the first naval ship bought by Congress—thanks to his acquaintance with a congressman. Jones was later given command of the *Providence*, where he earned a distinguished record.

A hero in the making. Promoted to captain and in command of the *Ranger*, Jones was sent to France. Sailing back and forth between France and the United States, he garnered quite a reputation. On his return trip to the United States, he managed to capture the British sloop *Drake*, taking many prisoners. Returning to France with seven "kills" and many prisoners to his credit, Jones was greeted as a hero. Later, in a journey around the British Isles, he captured seventeen ships, and then defeated the *Serapis* in an impressive bout.

Although political rivals blocked his promotion to admiral, Jones was awarded command of the *America*, the largest ship in the Navy (which was then under construction). Although Jones never took com-

John Paul Jones.

mand of the *America*, which was eventually turned over to the French, he received a gold medal from Congress and accepted an offer from Catherine the Great to serve in the Russian navy.

A proper burial and the sailor's biographer. Quite ill, Jones spent the last two years of his life in Paris. Buried in a French cemetery that was eventually taken over by housing, his body was shipped back to the

BIOGRAPHY AS FICTION

Augustus C. Buell also wrote the biographies of Sir William Johnson, William Penn, and Andrew Jackson. He claimed to have ancestors who had worked for, or who had known, all of the men he wrote about. All of Buell's biographies contain statements that are taken from documents that seem to have been made-to-order by the author himself: He freely invented letters, journal entries, books (usually described as quite rare), and even whole archives. Although Buell thanked the Library of Congress for making materials available to him, some scholars question whether the phoney biographer ever set foot in that library!

"MEMORIES" OF WAR

Buell's first publication, a book of memoirs of the Civil War, was a forgery. The writer claimed to have been a cannoneer at Gettysburg and elsewhere, and his vivid recollections were quoted in other anthologies of Civil War writings. Official records, however, told a different story: Buell did not enter the service until six weeks after the Battle of Gettysburg. What's more, he was never a cannoneer, and he wasn't even present at the battles he claimed to have lived through.

United States in 1905. Eight years later, his remains were buried in a specially constructed tomb at the U.S. Naval Academy in Annapolis, Maryland.

In 1900, Augustus C. Buell published a two-volume history titled *Paul Jones, Founder of the American Navy*. The writer's background, however, left something to be desired: His statements about his own history were often, in a word, inaccurate. In fact, Buell, who has been labeled a "fraudulent historian," manufactured the misinformation about Jones's role in the founding of the United States Navy.

Libraries in the sky. Scholars' reactions to Buell's biographies were mixed. Some praised his new "discoveries" while others concluded that he had located material that was no longer available. Librarians and archivists, however, had no luck finding the documents Buell claimed to have discovered in their libraries. The biographer, it seems, had provided himself with a clever "out": Because Buell claimed that one of his ancestors had known the subject of his biography, some scholars concluded that he must have consulted a family archive to research his books. The trouble was, no such archives existed.

In 1906, in the first exposé of Buell's biography of John Paul Jones, author Anna De Koven stated that the book

> is based upon a bare framework of truth ... but is padded with inventions of clever construction and unparalleled audacity. It contains reports of imaginary committees in Congress, invented letters from Washington, Franklin and Hewes, false letters and imaginary journals of Jones himself, false entries in the diaries of well-known persons such as Gouverneur Morris and the Duchesse d'Orleans, and quotations from others which existed only in Colonel Buell's imagination.... The bibliography ... is a masterpiece of invention, and is so shortsighted in its careless untruthfulness as to raise suspicion of the author's mental responsibility.

A clever dog. Samuel Eliot Morison, the author of the latest biography of Jones, devotes several pages to a list of Buell's false statements about Jones. About the writer, he says:

He found it easier to write Jones' letters himself than to use the genuine ones in the Library of Congress, which he never visited. How, then, did Buell acquire such a high reputation? He was a clever dog, wrote good salty prose and supported his statements by references to mythical sources and fictitious books, which gave his work an air of scholarly authenticity. Any librarian ... will do a service to posterity by reclassifying as fiction Buell's book [on Jones].

THE MAN WHO NEVER WAS

The Man Who Never Was is one of the most complex and clever military scams ever to fool enemy intelligence. The hoax, known as Operation Mincemeat, was masterminded by Ewen Montague during World War II.

Operation Mincemeat Fools German Military Intelligence!

Montague devised the hoax because the allied forces wanted to draw Nazi leader Adolf Hitler's, and Italian dictator Benito Mussolini's attention away from the upcoming allied invasion of Sicily, Italy. By making the Germans believe, however, that the invasion would take place from Greece and Sardinia, the allied forces would improve their odds for launching a successful attack.

The Man Who Was— Ewen Montague.

The plan called for the body of someone who had recently died of drowning or pneumonia and whose corpse could be used by British Military Intelligence. They would then dress the body in a British Marine officer's uniform, put the I.D. of Major William Martin on its body, and chain a briefcase containing "top secret information" to the body's wrist. The corpse was to wash ashore at Huelva, Spain, where active German agents mingled among the Spanish. The body would appear to have come from a ditched airplane and would be accompanied by a life raft.

A long search produced just such a body whose owner had died of pneumonia. After securing permission to use the body, military personnel stored the corpse in refrigeration until the Man Who Never Was was ready to make his public debut.

Since dropping the corpse from an airplane could damage it, Operation Mincemeat called for a submarine to release the body into the water. A torpedo-shaped canister was built so that it would release the body when opened. The canister also contained dry ice in order to drive out the oxygen that would speed up the body's decomposition.

Major Martin lands in Spain. After much difficulty, including getting the boots on the corpse's feet, among other things, the container with the body and briefcase was loaded aboard the submarine *Seraph*. The sub proceeded to the planned site, where the body was removed from the canister and "launched" toward shore. Days later, the naval attaché in Madrid sent a signal that Major Martin's body had been recovered off Huelva.

The British issued urgent requests through Spanish diplomatic channels to ensure the return of all the papers that Martin was carrying. All of the supposed courier's papers were returned—eventually. Tests showed, however, that the letters had been opened and resealed. Major Martin was buried in Spain, and his name and those of his plane's crew were added to the list of casualties for the week.

Mincemeat is swallowed whole. As the hoaxers had expected, the information in the secret letters was sent to Berlin, where the German intelligence service fell for it, hook, line, and sinker. A cablegram informed Winston Churchill (then a British statesman who later became prime minister), "Mincemeat swallowed whole." When the allies invaded Sicily, they encountered little in the way of resistance. Most of the defenses that the enemy had stationed in Sicily were relocated to the northern end of the island.

After the war, an examination of captured German naval intelligence files turned up a German translation of the secret letters that named Greece and Sardinia as the sites of the allied invasion. Admiral Doenitz, the commander in chief of the German navy, had initialled the letters to indicate that he had read them.

About that time, Doenitz met with Hitler, who did not think that the allied forces would attack Sicily first. Furthermore, General Rommel was sent from Italy to Greece to take charge of operations there—as if the Nazis were expecting an allied attack on Greece. In the end, Operation Mincemeat was a success, and it remains a classic military hoax.

Rules,
Regulations, and
Other Ruses

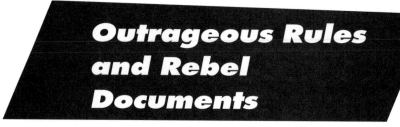

Outrageous Rules and Rebel Documents

THE BLUE LAWS OF CONNECTICUT

According to a so-called "Blue Law" of Connecticut, a man couldn't kiss his wife and a woman couldn't kiss her children on Sunday. Intended to regulate morality, the Blue Laws supposedly date back to the 1600s. More than a few of them, however, were hoaxes created in the eighteenth century by one Reverend Samuel Peters.

Connecticut Laws Punish Kissing on Sunday!

The Blue Laws got their name sometime around 1762, when someone assigned the name to an anonymous pamphlet and attached it to the laws of New Haven, Connecticut. The pamphlet, titled *The Real Advantages Which Ministers and People May Enjoy, Especially in the Colonies, by Conforming to the Church of England*, was probably written by Reverend Noah Wells of Stamford, Connecticut.

Actual examples of the Blue laws, however, were never published until 1782, when Reverend Samuel Peters produced his *General History of Connecticut*. Published in London, Peters's book is the only source that lists the Blue Laws—something that makes the experts more than a little suspicious.

As a matter of fact, the Reverend Samuel Peters was somewhat of a suspicious character. An acquaintance called him factually unreliable, especially when it came to storytelling. Peters even made up part of his family history, claiming that the early Connecticut settler Hugh Peters was his brother. And the Good Reverend's dubious degrees—a doctorate of law and a doctorate of divinity—were more evidence that he was "factually unreliable."

Rules, Regulations, and Other Ruses

Peters punishes the state of Connecticut. Peters was accused of attempting to punish the state of Connecticut by writing its history. He intended his book for a British audience, but they recognized that it was not a factual account; few people paid attention to Peters's so-called "history." In fact, a critique of the book in the *Monthly Review* went so far as to state "we do not hesitate to pronounce it altogether unworthy of the public attention."

Peters had a number of things to say about the New Haven colony laws.

> They consist of a vast multitude and were properly termed *Blue Laws*, i.e. *bloody laws*; for they were all sanctified with excommunication, confiscation, fines, banishment, whippings, cutting off of the ears, burning the tongue, and death.... And did not similar laws still [in 1782] prevail over New England as the common law of the country, I would have left them in silence.

Again, Peters was being unreliable: There were no such laws in 1782, and the term "Blue Laws" did not come from "bloody laws."

The Source of the Blue Laws. Peters called his Blue Laws the code of the New Haven colony. There actually was a code of New Haven laws from 1655, but it did not contain any of the Blue Laws. *The Connecticut Code of 1650* is often cited as Peters's source, although he never cited any source.

The true source of Peters's laws seems to have been his imagination, although little is known about his motivation. Peters's laws have been reprinted several times, and—even today—few people know that the Blue Laws of Connecticut were an elaborate hoax.

THE COMMUNIST RULES FOR REVOLUTION

The Communist Rules for Revolution—a set of ten rules that was written as official Communist policy—was supposed to have been "captured" by the allied forces in Dusseldorf, Germany, in 1919. Since then, it has been reproduced time and again, especially in right-wing (ultra-conservative) publications.

Communist Rules Corrupt Young and Destroy Democracy!

In 1981, *Chicago Tribune* columnist Bob Greene was tired of receiving copies of *The Rules*. He decided to investigate its authenticity, and contacted a number of historians and scholars who were experts on Communism and Soviet history. All of the experts said that *The Rules* was a fake and had never existed as Communist policy. Additionally, it wasn't composed in 1919 by the early Communists; it was probably composed sometime around 1950.

The following is one version of *The Communist Rules for Revolution*:

1. Corrupt the young. Get them away from religion. Get them interested in sex. Make them superficial. Destroy their ruggedness.

2. Get control of all means of publicity.

3. Get people's minds off their government by focusing their attention on athletics, sexy books and plays, and other trivialities.

4. Divide the people into hostile groups by constantly harping on controversial matters of no importance.

5. Destroy the people's faith in their natural leaders by holding the latter up to contempt, ridicule, and obloquy [bad repute].

Chicago Tribune columnist Bob Greene.

6. Always preach true democracy, but seize power as fast and as ruthlessly as possible.

7. By encouraging government extravagance, destroy its credit and produce fear of inflation with rising prices and general discontent.

8. Foment [stir up] unnecessary strikes in vital industries, encourage civil disorders, and foster a lenient and soft attitude on the part of government toward such disorders.

9. By specious [deceptive] argument cause the breakdown of the old moral virtues, honesty, sobriety, continence, faith in the pledged word, ruggedness.

10. Cause the registration of all firearms on some pretext, with a view to confiscating them and leaving the population helpless.

The experts agree: *The Rules* is a fake. Professor Davis Joravsky of Northwestern University in Evanston, Illinois, was one of the scholars Greene consulted. Joravsky stated that many of the rules were contrary to true Communist beliefs and that they "are an obvious fabrication. They are not Communist in their origin."

Professor Jeffrey Brooks at the University of Chicago agreed that *The Rules* was "impossible and improbable" as Communist policy. And Arcadius Kahan, a professor of economics and history at the University of Chicago, added that a person would have to be "an idiot" to believe that *The Rules* had been published or written by the Communists.

If *The Communist Rules for Revolution* were, indeed, an authentic captured document, it should have been filed in the U.S. National Archives; however, when the archives were searched, no such rules were found. In fact, nothing about the "Communist Master Plan" suggests that it was anything but a hoax.

THE MECKLENBURG DECLARATION

It is widely believed that the Declaration of Independence, proclaimed on July 4, 1776, was the first attempt to declare America free of European colonial powers.

The Mecklenburg Declaration was supposedly announced on May 20, 1775, in Mecklenburg County, North Carolina. It was published in an issue of the *Cape Fear Mercury*, a newspaper of the area, in an issue that has not survived. Some people claim, based on a version reconstructed from memory, that the Mecklenburg Declaration—written more than 100 years before the Declaration of Independence—called for American independence from Great Britain.

The Declaration of Independence Was Old Hat in 1776!

In 1800, John McKnitt Alexander, who participated in the meetings that led to the "resolves" produced at Mecklenburg, made notes from his memory of the declaration. His notes placed the date of the declaration as May 20, 1775, although the series of resolves were adopted in Mecklenburg County on May 31, 1775.

During the winter of 1818-19, Congress spent much time discussing whether the people of Mecklenburg had declared themselves free of England before July 4, 1776. Eventually the text of the Mecklenburg Declaration was produced for inspection. The entire text of the declaration is as follows, except for the list of signers and a description of the circumstances:

1. *Resolved*, That whoever directly or indirectly abetted or in any way, form or manner, countenanced the unchartered and dangerous invasion of our rights, as claimed by Great Britain, is an enemy to this country—to America—and to the inherent and inalienable rights of man.

2. *Resolved*, That we the citizens of Mecklenburg County, do hereby dissolve the political bands which have connected us to the Mother Country, and hereby absolve ourselves from all allegiance to the British Crown, and abjure all political connection, contract, or as-

sociation, with that nation, who have wantonly trampled on our rights and liberties—and inhumanly shed the innocent blood of American patriots at Lexington.

3. *Resolved,* That we do hereby declare ourselves a free and independent people, are, and of right ought to be a sovereign and self-governing Association, under the control of no power other than that of our God and the General Government of the Congress; to the maintenance of which independence, we solemnly pledge to each other, our mutual co-operation, our lives, our fortunes, and our most sacred honor.

4. *Resolved,* That as we acknowledge the existence and control of no law or legal officer, civil or military, within this county, we do hereby ordain and adopt, as a rule of life, all, each and every of our former laws, wherein, nevertheless, the Crown of Great Britain can never be considered as holding rights, privileges, immunities, or authority therein.

5. *Resolved*, That it is further decreed, that all, each and every military officer in this country, is hereby reinstated to his former command and authority, he acting conformably to these regulations. And that every member present of this delegation shall henceforth be a civil officer, viz, a Justice of the Peace, in the character of a "Committeeman," to issue process, hear and determine all matters of controversy, according to said adopted laws, and to preserve peace, and union, and harmony, in said county, and to use every exertion to spread the love of country and fire of freedom throughout America, until a more general and organized government be established in this province.

A document ahead of its time. The declaration was carried to the Philadelphia Congress, with a letter addressed to the three North Carolina representatives. Although the individual members of Congress agreed with the sentiments of the declaration, they decided that it was too early to present the entire document to the House.

In 1819, all of this information was made public and was circulated in newspapers around the country. When John Adams noticed an article about the declaration in his local Massachusetts newspaper, he wrote to Thomas Jefferson to express his surprise.

Jefferson responded that he thought the document was not authentic; he based his opinion on his inability to find evidence from the 1775 period and on the fact that there was no mention of the document in the eighteenth century. Adams—who at first had been inclined to believe the declaration to be genuine—was convinced by Jefferson's reply.

A committee is appointed. Jefferson's opinion became widely known through the 1829 publication of the first edition of his *Works of Thomas Jefferson*. Jefferson's dismissal of the document upset North Carolinians, who accepted the Mecklenburg Declaration as authentic.

In an attempt to meet Jefferson's demand for additional proof, the North Carolina legislature appointed a committee in 1830-31 to "examine, collate, and arrange" evidence about the declaration. In 1831 the committee reported that the declaration was genuine.

Shortly after this report appeared, Peter Force, who was working on his book *American Archives*, discovered a proclamation issued by the royal governor of North Carolina on August 8, 1775. Governor Josiah Martin stated that he had seen:

> a most infamous publication in the *Cape Fear Mercury* importing to be resolves of a set of people styling themselves a committee for the county of Mecklenburg, most traitorously declaring the entire dissolution of the laws, government, and constitution of this country, and setting up

a system of rule and regulation repugnant to the laws and subversive of his majesty's government.

Force also found the text of the preamble and the first four resolutions in the *Massachusetts Spy or American Oracle of Liberty* of July 12, 1775. Over the following years, other supporting documents were found.

The text of the resolutions, however, was different from the version reconstructed from memory: It was broader, and applied to all of the colonies. The version of the Resolves that were adopted on May 31, 1775, took the following form:

WHEREAS by an Address presented to his Majesty by both Houses of Parliament, in February last, the American colonies are declared to be in a state of actual rebellion, we conceive, that all laws and commissions confirmed by, or derived from the authority of the King or Parliament, are annulled and vacated, and the former civil constitution of these colonies, for the present, wholly suspended. To provide, in some degree, for the exigencies [demands] of this country, in the present alarming period, we deem it proper and necessary to pass the following Resolves, viz:

I. That all commissions, civil and military, heretofore granted by the Crown, to be exercised in these colonies, are null and void, and the constitution of each particular colony wholly suspended.

II. That the Provincial Congress of each province, under the direction of the great Continental Congress, is invested with all legislative and executive powers within their respective provinces; and that no other legislative or executive power does, or can exist, at this time in any of these colonies.

III. As all former laws are now suspended in this province, and the Congress have not provided others, we judge it to be necessary, for better preservation of good order, to form certain rules and regulations for the internal government of this county, until laws shall be provided for us by the Congress.

IV. That the inhabitants of this county do meet on a certain day appointed by this Committee, and having formed themselves into nine companies (to wit) eight in the county, and one in the town of Charlotte, do chuse [sic] a Colonel and other military officers, who shall hold and exercise their several powers by virtue of this choice, and independent of the Crown of Great Britain, and former constitution of this province.

V. That for the better preservation of the peace and administration of justice, each of those companies do chuse [sic] from their own body, two discreet freeholders, who shall be empowered, each by himself and singly, to decide and determine all matters of controversy, arising within said company, under the sum of twenty shillings; and jointly and together, all controversies under the sum of forty shillings; yet so as that their decisions may admit of appeal to the Convention of the Select-Men of the county; and also that any one of these men, shall have power to examine and commit to confinement persons accused of petit larceny.

VI. That those two Select-Men, thus chosen, do jointly and together chuse [sic] from the body of their particular company, two persons properly qualified to act as Constables, who may assist them in the execution of their office.

VII. That upon the complaint of any persons to either of these Select-Men, he do issue his warrant, directed to the Constable, commanding him to bring the aggressor before him or them, to answer said complaint.

VIII. That these eighteen Select-Men, thus appointed, do meet every third Thursday in January, April, July, and October, at the Court-House, in Charlotte, to hear and determine all matters of controversy, for sums exceeding forty shillings, also appeals; and in cases of felony, to commit the person or persons convicted thereof to close confinement, until the Provincial Congress shall provide and establish laws and modes of proceeding in all such cases.

Articles IX through XVI deal with trials, debtors, taxes, and a militia. The concluding articles follow:

XVII. That any person refusing to yield obedience to the above Resolves, shall be considered equally criminal, and liable to the same punishment, as the offenders above last mentioned [held to be dealt with "as prudence may direct."].

XVIII. That these Resolves be in full force and virtue, until instructions from the Provincial congress, regulating the jurisprudence of the province, shall provide otherwise, or the legislative body of Great-Britain, resign its unjust and arbitrary pretentions with respect to America.

XIX. That the eight militia companies in the county, provide themselves with proper arms and accoutrements, and hold themselves in readiness to execute the commands and directions of the General Congress of this province and this Committee.

XX. That the Committee appoint Colonel Thomas Polk, and Doctor Joseph Kennedy, to purchase 300 lb. of powder, 600 lb. of lead, 1000 flints, for use of the militia of this county, and deposit the same in such place as the Committee may hereafter direct.

Different resolutions. *This* set of resolves is very different from the other: These resolutions deal largely with the local administration of law and order. While they express some dissatisfaction with British administration of the colony, they do not call for independence from Great Britain. The first declaration was much stronger in this respect, and actually called for the political "bands" connecting Great Britain and North Carolina to be dissolved.

Today, those who believe the Mecklenburg declarations to be authentic say that the May 31 Resolves were never adopted in that form; rather, they were amended on May 20 into a declaration of independence. Additionally, those who claim to have been present support the claim that the declaration proclaimed independence from Great Britain. The first document of the period that mentions the declaration is a Charleston newspaper; the June 16, 1775 issue of *The South-Carolina Gazette and Country Journal* gives the full text of the Mecklenburg Resolves adopted on May 31, 1775. These do not declare independence from Great Britain (see the second set of text above).

No such view of independence. The first set of text above is a sort of declaration of independence from Great Britain. But the papers of then-Governor Martin of North Carolina suggest that he wasn't aware of the resolutions: More than a month after the declaration was supposedly published, Martin issued a proclamation at Fort Johnston that revealed no knowledge of the Mecklenburg Resolves.

Another eyewitness to the signing dismissed the document as a declaration of independence. James Iredell of North Carolina was an associate justice of the U.S. Supreme Court who was present at the North Carolina events in 1775; yet, in 1776, he said "we [North Carolina] have never taken any one step which really indicated such a view [independence]."

A failing memory. The only source of the first version of the Mecklenburg Declaration is the copy of the declaration that John McKnitt Alexander made in 1800, from memory, after his house burned down. These Resolves are very different from the second version of the declaration.

The evidence does not suggest that there was ever a Mecklenburg Declaration of Independence—certainly not before our country's forefathers penned the Congressional Declaration of Independence. In truth, the first version of the Mecklenburg Declaration was probably the product of a poor memory, constructed from Alexander's vague recollection of the second version of the document.

THE *OATH OF A FREEMAN*

The first recorded piece of printed material in the United States was a single sheet, or "broadside," on which the *Oath of a Freeman* was printed. The *Oath* was printed by Stephen Daye at Cambridge, Massachusetts in 1638-39. Although no known first-run copies of the *Oath* exist, the text has survived through later reprints. Every freeman in Massachusetts had to swear the oath to attain full citizenship. Since the oath could only be sworn in person before an official, the printed oath was probably used by local officials to read to the petitioner.

Forger of Oath of a Freeman Jailed!

Mark Hofmann, born in Utah in 1954, bought and sold Mormon historical books, documents, and currency. In 1985—with a number of significant finds to his credit—he contacted a New York City rare book dealer to inform him that he had found something that answered the description of the *Oath of a Freeman.*

In truth, Hofmann was involved in a large-scale document forgery scheme. The way in which the *Oath of a Freeman* was forged was ingenious. Each letter of the words needed to form the text of the *Oath* was cut from a facsimile (exact copy) edition of the *Bay Psalm Book,* which was printed by Daye two years later than the supposed broadside publication date. The words were enclosed in a border also cut from the *Bay Psalm Book.*

After taking a photograph of the mocked-up version, the forger made a metal etching of the photograph. The type images on the plate were then carefully filed or sanded to resemble uneven inking, in order to imitate Daye's usually poor inking. The ink was made from carbon black, obtained by burning paper from the 1600s—in case potential buyers wanted to perform carbon dating tests on the document. Hofmann used ink that he made from a 1600s recipe, and he was careful not to use tap water in its formula.

Hofmann also made sure that the *Oath* showed type "bite" (an impression made by the type on the paper) showing through the back of the paper; how this was accomplished is unclear. This "bite" made it appear that the document had been printed by letterpress and not by offset printing. The paper used was cut from books of the 1620-40 period found at the University of Utah and Brigham Young University libraries.

Hofmann made only one major error in his *Oath* forgery, and it was not noticed until *after* he had secured several hundred thousand dollars in advances for the *Oath* and other documents. It seems Hofmann contracted the word "established" to "stablished," something that Daye *never* did.

INDEX

Boldface indicates entrants

Sherby, Sidney 17
Shroud of Turin 36-41
Shroud of Turin Research Project
(STURP) 40
Smith, E. J. 25
Smith, Grafton Elliot 6
Smith, Paul Jordan 192
Smithsonian Institution 67
The Soal and Levy Hoaxes 56-59
Soal, S. G. 56, 58-59
Soccer 216-217
Sollas, William Johnson 6
Space Vehicle 26-28
Spaulding, Albert 210
Spector, Mark 118
Spiritualist Mediums 50-56, 147
Sports Illustrated 213-214
Spurling, Christian 15
St. Barbe, Guy 8
Stephen, Adrian 90-92
Stephen, Virginia 90
Stewart, Gloria 58
Stratton, Charles Sherwood 204
Stride, Elizabeth 145
Subliminal Messages (see Backward
Masking)
Summerlin, William T. 116, 118-119
Surgeon's Photo 13-15
Swoboda, Herman 123, 124

T

Tamara Rand Hoax 74-75
Tavernier, John Baptiste 65
Teilhard de Chardin, Pierre 6, 8
Teltscher, Alfred 123, 124
Terry, James 58
Tesla, Nikola 26, 131-132
Test Tube Experiments 120
Thommen, George S. 123
Thumb, Tom 204-205
Tighe, Virginia (see Bridey Murphy)
Tuck, Dick 138-139
Tutankhamen, King 67-71
Twentieth-Century Art Forger 188-192
**Two Hoaxers: Smith and de Hory
192-193**

U

U.S. Naval Academy 94
UFOtographs 21
Unidentified Flying Objects (UFO's) 16-28
"The Unparalleled Adventures of One
Hans Pfaall" 176

V

Van Meegeren, Hans 188-191
Varo Company 17
Venusian Spacecraft 20
Vermeer, Jan 189-191
Victor Notaro's Soccer Stories 214-215
Viking Hoaxes 84-87
Vinland Map 84-85
Vokey, Don 196
Vortigern and Rowena 179-180

W

Wahlgren, Erik 86
Wallace, Alfred R. 178
Ware, Robert 35
Warren, Lavinia (Minnie) 204
Weber, William 63, 64
Weiner, Joseph 6, 8
Wells, Noah 98
Wetherell, Ian 15
Wetherell, Maraduke 15
The Wildman 12
William of Malmsbury 132
Wilson, Robert K. 13-15
Winer, Richard 165
Winlock, Herbert E. 69
Winston, Harry 66, 67
Witchcraft 169-170
Woodhall, Edwin T. 148
Woodhead, Samuel 7
Woodward, Adam Smith 6
World Cup 216, 217
Wright Brothers 132
Wynne, Charles 53

Y

Yeti 8, 9